Now Say *This*

Heather Turgeon, MFT, and Julie Wright, MFT, are psychotherapists who run a Los Angeles and New York City–based sleep and parenting practice. They offer sleep consultations all over the world for babies, toddlers, and school-age children, as well as parenting consultations and individual therapy. Their first book, *The Happy Sleeper: The Science-Backed Guide to Helping Your Baby Get a Good Night's Sleep*, is a top-selling sleep book that parents have called "life changing" and "a breath of fresh air." Featured on outlets like NPR, Heather and Julie bring together science and emotional attunement to solve parenting dilemmas.

Heather Turgeon is a psychotherapist who specializes in sleep and parenting. Her writing has appeared in *The New York Times* and *The Washington Post* and she frequently speaks at parenting centers and schools. She lives in Los Angeles with her husband and two kids.

Julie Wright divides her time between Los Angeles and New York City. She is the creator of the Wright Mommy and Me, one of Los Angeles's best-known mommy and me programs. She has specialized training and experience in the 0–3 years, having interned at the Cedars-Sinai Early Childhood Center and LA Child Guidance Clinic. She travels to LA often and has a son in college.

Now Say *This*

the right words to solve every parenting dilemma

The 3-step approach to effective communication

Heather Turgeon, MFT,
and Julie Wright, MFT

SCRIBE

Melbourne • London

Scribe Publications
2 John Street, Clerkenwell, London, WC1N 2ES, United Kingdom
18–20 Edward St, Brunswick, Victoria 3056, Australia

This edition published by arrangement with TarcherPerigee, an imprint of Penguin
Publishing Group, a division of Penguin Random House LLC

Published by Scribe 2018

Illustration credits: Pages 10, 53, 106, 114, 132, 205, 242, 282, 309: Ben Hansford
Pages 12, 27, 33, 51, 58, 109, 113: Kristen Barnhart
Pages 69, 311: Jack Sheehy

Printed and bound in the UK by CPI Group (UK) Ltd, Croydon CR0 4YY

Scribe Publications is committed to the sustainable use of natural resources
and the use of paper products made responsibly from those resources.

9781911617501 (UK edition)
9781925713350 (ANZ edition)
9781925693119 (e-book)

CiP data records for this title are available from the National Library of Australia and
the British Library.

scribepublications.co.uk
scribepublications.com.au

Contents

Introduction

I have the best intentions to be a good parent. I start the day ready to be supermom, ready to be positive and patient and say the right thing, but when no one listens, the shoes don't go on, my son is mean to his sister . . . I just lose it.

A mom of two little kids said this to us one day. Well-meaning and thoughtful, she was trying her best to be the parent she'd always envisioned she'd be, but every day she felt as if she was falling short. The negative tone, nagging, and power struggles in the house reached a breaking point one afternoon, when she grabbed a dollhouse and threw it out the back door in frustration. Her kids were horrified and so was she. She called us.

We hear dilemmas like this every day in our groups and private practice. These are loving moms and dads who want the best for their kids. They want the family to be close, but instead of fostering harmony and collaboration they often feel like drill sergeants, issuing no's, yelling, and time-outing—or pleading, negotiating, and ultimately feeling like their kids run the show.

What we realized is that these dilemmas actually happen for a good reason, which is that *empathy is on the rise.* Parents are aware of how important it is to be connected, understanding, and warm to their kids. Decades of research has shown that these natural instincts to comfort and listen lead to stronger relationships, higher achievement, and lower anxiety and depression. Parents have been told to be positive, that they're "not supposed" to yell, bribe, or threaten, and that traditional actions like spanking and punishments are detrimental.

The problem is that, in some ways, this has created a vacuum for parents, in which the standard tools have been taken away, but not necessarily replaced with something tangible. Moms and dads have the best of intentions to be kind and empathic but end up feeling indulgent and so frustrated that they eventually resort to yelling and punishing after all.

In our practice, we've seen a clear need for a balanced approach to discipline (from the Latin word, *disciplina*, or "teaching," not punishment), one that is both empathic and effective. Not only that, we knew that to really help parents, our system had to be easy to remember and follow. The beauty is that our three-step, or "ALP" approach, can be applied to any difficult moment in life, as you'll see through our coaching in this book. Our clients apply it to parenting issues (like tantrums, not listening, and sibling conflicts), and as they practice they see its ripple effects in their partner relationship, work dilemmas, and beyond. They tell us over and over again that the three-step model changes their whole outlook on being a parent. Rather than dread difficult moments, they feel confident and optimistic. They know what to do and say to be effective, all the while nurturing a close relationship to their child and keeping their eyes on their bigger goals as a parent.

Your Child Is Capable

You may have noticed: parenting topics can be polarizing. We saw this for years on the subject of baby sleep, which led us to write our first book, *The Happy Sleeper*. The subject of discipline has the same either/or perception problem. One side swears by strict rules and consequences for "bad behavior" and believes that permissive parenting leads to unruly, entitled kids. The other side thinks that empathy and warmth are the key to teaching, and that very strict discipline causes kids to fear, rather than trust, their parents. We see these "discipline wars" every day in our work with families—sometimes even *within* the same family! Whichever camp they're in, though, most parents tell us that something is missing. When they're very strict, they end up feeling guilty and worry they're missing a deeper connection to their kids. When they try to empathize and be flexible, they often feel ineffective and resentful. It's no surprise that more than 70 percent of parents say that discipline is the hardest part of raising a child.

Rather than choosing one side, research tells us that the best outcomes and highest satisfaction in families come from choosing both. ALP is the way to accomplish this. In order to have both, we start by taking our clients back to some simple but profound premises about children:

Your child is capable.

She wants to listen and learn.

He's wired for empathy.

She wants to help.

He wants to feel like an important part of your family.

You're on the same team.

When we show our moms and dads this list, some nod as if to say, "of course," while others shake their heads in disagreement (still others crack jokes). But not only are these statements true—as shown by decades of child development research and clinical experience—they dramatically change how you interact with your child on a daily basis, including in difficult moments. When you adopt these principles (as we'll guide you to do in this book, starting with babies as young as seven months), you'll see how traditional tactics like rewards and punishments do not make sense and actually work against you. You'll see "misbehavior" as a sign that your child is working on a developmental skill. You'll understand how to collaborate with your child, and your job as a parent becomes very clear, logical, and doable.

Many other clinicians and scholars have written about empathic parenting and delved deeply into the theory and science that support this way of being with our kids. Our hope is that this book serves as a practical "how-to," an easy-to-follow guide that brings all of these remarkable ideas into a format that busy parents can begin to use right away.

Why "Now Say This . . ."?

One day, we were leading a workshop for parents at a local preschool. Talking about engaging cooperation at bedtime (a concept from *The Happy Sleeper*) we said to the audience,

"For example, you might say this . . ."

Suddenly, the parents grabbed their notebooks and pens and looked at us expectantly. Yes, they had been engaged during the class, but now they were about to hear us say the actual words, demonstrate the actions, and convey the tone—and that piqued their interest even more.

Words are powerful. Pages and pages of explanations and theory can often be artfully conveyed by a pause, the right body language and tone, and one or two sentences. When we started to work on a book about setting limits with empathy—a topic we've taught to thousands of families—our intention was to be as clear and helpful as possible. At first we weren't sure what to think about words and scripts being the centerpiece of this book. Communication is an art form, not an exact science, so we would never want to imply that *our* words are the *only* words. Each family has its own language, mannerisms, and cultural context.

Quickly we realized, though, that parents love examples. They crystalize general ideas into actionable ones. In our Mommy and Me groups, parents say that empathic communication is their favorite topic, and the ALP model has changed the way they talk to their babies, toddlers, and children for years to come. We brainstorm with our clients, "What could you have said in that moment to let her know you really understand?" or "Imagine the words *you* would like to hear when *you're* upset." They love this exercise, and often they jot down notes and say, "Oh, can you repeat that!" They come back to us all the time with sentiments like, "My child let me in on something deeper about her problem, I had no idea!"

The examples and scripts in this book will allow you to change the way you talk to your kids starting *today*. By the time you've read through, you will have added your own personal nuances. If you have a baby, we're so happy you've picked this book up, because it's easiest to start early, and how you talk to her now will forever change your relationship.

Parents are often shocked by the effectiveness of this approach. They're shocked by how ready their kids are to become competent, well-meaning, creative, cooperative parts of the family, and how changing the tone and words reveal this. We are reaching beyond "effective," though. We want to help you nurture a child who is kind to herself and others, who is confident and independent, and who understands what is fair and right. A child who trusts that you are always there to listen and guide, no matter how much you might not approve of her behavior. Kids are not shaped by external forces to be "good"; as parents we simply nurture and reveal that they already are.

The shoes will go on, *and* you'll feel closer in the process.

How to Use This Book

Chapter 1: This chapter covers fundamental concepts and outlines the three-step, or ALP, model of communication. It's important to read this chapter because the principles in it (such as defining your bigger goals as a parent, shifting how you view your child's capabilities, and looking beneath the surface) make the ALP model successful.

Chapter 2: This chapter gives you "proactive tools" to help keep the family in balance, making it less likely that you'll be stuck in a difficult moment in the first place. With the concepts in this chapter, the tone of the day can change and difficult moments may be less likely to happen. The ratio of enjoying each other to conflicts will go up with these preventative tools.

Chapters 3–8: In these chapters you learn how to apply the ALP model in various types of difficult moments (tantrums, hitting, not listening, sibling conflict, screen time, and bedtime).

To get started, read chapter 1 and review the proactive tools. Then you can jump straight to the issue most relevant to your family.

For supplemental tools, please visit nowsaythisbook.com and thehappysleeper.com.

CHAPTER ONE

Three Steps for Communicating in Difficult Moments

Unless I'm responding with my whole self—unless, in fact, I'm willing to be changed *by you—I'm probably not really listening.*

—**Alan Alda**

Do any of these scenarios sound familiar?

Your kids will not brush their teeth or put on their shoes. You feel as though you're always nagging. You eventually snap and raise your voice, and then feel bad later.

After asking your preschooler five times to turn off her iPad, her only reaction is to have a meltdown on your living room floor.

Your children tease, provoke, and even hit each other. You repeatedly insist, "be nice to your brother/sister," but the only peace comes from separating them.

Your school-age child resists and negotiates with you over unfinished homework. You try to explain the importance of hard work. He gets mad and slams his bedroom door.

Your three-year-old has an epic tantrum in a restaurant because she wants your phone. You'd like to have a nice family dinner but instead each child, as well as your partner, ends up on a device.

Despite your patient assurances, your eight-month-old does not cease crying, squirming, and kicking on the changing table as you struggle to change her diaper.

Though you have clearly said it's time for sleeping, your toddler is running, giggling, throwing toys—anything except heading to bed.

As a parent, these are moments when you're just trying to get by. You want your child to listen, to stop crying or complaining, to get with the program and keep moving.

But there's a voice in the back of your head telling you that being a parent is about more than getting by. You are raising a human being. You are in charge of guiding and supporting a budding little person. When we ask the parents we work with what they wish for their child—what kind of person they hope their child grows into—the most popular answers are:

Feels loved and is loving

Is confident

Has a moral compass

Works hard and is high achieving

Is self-disciplined

Feels peaceful and positive most of the time

Is self-aware

Is connected to family

Has empathy for self and others

When you think about your bigger goals as a parent, it puts the everyday struggles in a different light. Yes, you want the shoes to go on, the crying to stop, and the homework to get done. But ultimately, you want something deeper. You want a loving, strong connection with your child. You want to teach her, to support her growing brain to think creatively, to cultivate empathy, and to develop problem-solving skills and self-esteem.

That's what this book is about. There's a lot of advice out there about "discipline"—promising to get your child to do what you say—but we want more for you. The way you communicate in difficult moments—how you listen, your body language, and your choice of words and actions—will steadily influence how your child feels about herself, relationships, and the world around her.

The Win-Win of Good Parenting

The science of child development and parenting is complex and nuanced. Of course it is; humans are infinitely complex creatures, and no two relationships are the same. But thankfully, research does converge on a through line of what makes for a good parent and a well-adjusted, successful child. It's a mix of characteristics that might, at first, seem like they don't work together. You might even see them as opposites—but in this book, we'll show you how they fit together perfectly. This "gold standard" of parenting has been described in different ways by clinicians and scholars over the years: warmth *and* high expectations, empathy *and* clear limits, kind *and* consistent. Studies of children who are parented this way show them to be confident, caring, self-regulated, high-achieving little people.

No doubt, you work at this balance every day. You have mountains of love for your child, and yet you also want her to know that you are the parent, and you are in charge. This is the win-win.

WIN	WIN
Warmth	High expectations
Empathy	Clear limits
Kind	Consistent

We're going to show you how the win-win will not only help you solve your problems in the moment, it will lead you to your bigger goals. In fact, you'll be surprised to see, with the methods in this book, that the ideal stance is to be firmly planted in *both* sides at the same time. They work together. Most parenting struggles come from a breakdown on one side of the win-win. We see it every day in our practice: A dad who has high demands for his son but cannot accept his difficult emotions. A mom with endless warmth who cannot hold limits and feels walked all over by her kids. In the media and in your social circles, you hear one side of the same dilemma over and over again. Some people think we should respond more sensitively to babies and kids to build a secure attachment. Others think children don't have enough structure and that parents are too soft and lenient.

Decades of research supports the "win-win" of good parenting. Studies show that parenting styles high on **responsiveness** (warmth, sensitivity) and **expectations** (demands that parents put on a child to integrate into the family and society) are linked to children's higher school achievement. When parents teach and encourage collaboration in a warm emotional environment, kids learn more than when parents use rewards and punishments.

Three Steps, and Words, for the Win-Win

We are here to teach you how to have both, as we've done with thousands of families using our three-step model of communication.

With this three-step approach—attune, limit set, and problem solve, or "ALP"—we will teach you how to maintain the win-win. Our families tell us over and over how empowered and confident the

ATTUNE → LIMIT SET → PROBLEM SOLVE

three steps make them feel. They tell us that they spend less time struggling and more time enjoying their kids. ALP allows them not just to get through difficult moments, but to connect and deepen their family relationships.

Once you understand the *why* of the ALP approach, we're going to take it a step further—we're going to give you the actual words. You don't have to repeat them exactly (in fact, over time we hope you create your own!). The scripts in this book give you a concrete place to begin.

With these tools as your starting point, we want to *change the way you think about your role as a parent.* We're going to challenge you to lean into difficult moments rather than fearing them, and, even in the heat of your most frustrating interactions, practice responses that keep the win-win in place. The rewards for your family will last a lifetime.

Three Premises of ALP

ALP is not just a technique, it's a way of seeing children and family relationships that is based on these premises:

- Your child is capable.
- Difficult behavior is the "tip of the iceberg."
- Big emotions are like storms.

These concepts are key to the effectiveness of ALP.

Premise #1:
Your Child Is Capable and Built for Good

The premise of our first book, *The Happy Sleeper*, is a simple truth: *Your baby is built to sleep. Sleep is natural.* It's a message that resonates with parents because it helps them believe in their babies and give them credit for what they're capable of doing.

So here's a secret that helps our parents change the way they communicate: *children are built for good.* It may not seem like it, in that moment when your toddler smacks her brother with a hard clump of Play-Doh or ruins a thoughtfully prepared meal by kicking her plate of spaghetti to the floor. But it's true. When we say children are built for good, what we mean is that kids are wired with the potential for empathy, for kindness, to learn from experiences, and to get along with others.

BABY SKILLS

The littlest of babies have a moral sense—this is the take-away suggested by child development research. Scientists find that babies as young as three to six months can judge the rightness or wrongness of others' actions, and they gravitate to the right or positive ones. For example, when six-month-olds watch a puppet *help* another, versus a puppet that is *unhelpful*, they quickly develop a preference for the helpful puppet. They look at that puppet longer and reach out to play with it. Babies are not blank slates, they already have a sense of morality and a tendency to look toward what is good.

We don't have to micromanage or muscle them, nor do we have to impose morality on them. They have natural tendencies toward learning and cooperation. We can give them space to test and make mistakes with our guidance and modeling. When children act out, they are not "being bad," they're working on a developmental skill, like emotional regulation or frustration tolerance, or they're trying to communicate with us in the as-yet only way they know how.

The premise that your child is good will inform how you interpret tough behaviors and stuck moments. Rather than responding with threats or punishments, you can see your child as a small person with good intentions, figuring out a big world. You have an opportunity to understand, set limits, and guide. The parents we work with tell us over and over that this helps them feel more patient. They shift from worrying there's something wrong, to seeing emotions and difficult behaviors both as normal and as opportunities for growth.

UNHELPFUL/ TRADITIONAL	HELPFUL/ACCURATE
Children are naturally selfish.	Children have an innate capacity for empathy.
Children don't like responsibility.	Children like to be needed and seen as capable.
Children don't know right from wrong, they need to be rewarded and punished to learn.	Children have a natural sense of right and wrong. We help this to grow from the inside out.
Children aren't capable of reasoning.	Children are capable of reasoning and we nourish it by explaining and talking respectfully.
If we don't control them, children will misbehave.	When kids "misbehave" it tells us they need support, explanation, or are working on a developmental skill.
Kids need tough love. That's what makes a good parent.	How we treat our children affects how they treat everyone else.

UNHELPFUL/ TRADITIONAL	HELPFUL/ACCURATE
Kids need to be forced or controlled to do the right thing.	*Children have a desire to be part of a group and to be helpful, important, and integral in the family.*
Kids can't resolve conflicts. We need to do it for them.	*Kids can often come up with good solutions on their own.*

Premise #2:
Difficult Behavior Is the Tip of the Iceberg

Let's imagine a typical evening scenario: the kids are "winding down" for bed, which means they're laughing maniacally, running around the house, ignoring Mom's repeated "brush your teeth" demands, and, with each passing minute, appearing magically to be moving farther away from bed rather than closer to it.

What do you immediately see in this scenario? You see noncompliance, unruly behavior, maybe even disrespectfulness. In that case Mom, in her frustration at being ignored, might yell,

Get your teeth brushed—now—or no stories and straight to bed!

This is Mom responding to the "tip of the iceberg."

Now, what if we told you that Mom has been working all day and the kids have just come from a playdate with friends. Homework is finally finished and it's past their regular bedtime. What do you see in this scenario now? You might see a need to connect with Mom, a feeling of missing her (funny way to express it, right?). You see the hyperactivity of sleepy kids. Given that insight, now Mom might say,

I see silly people running all over the place here. Hey, everyone, urgent cuddle 911! I've missed you guys so much today. I'm excited to see what happens in the next chapter of that book we started last night. So teeth and then meet me on the couch!

In the first example, Mom talks to the "tip of the iceberg," whereas in the second example she looks at the part of the iceberg that is beneath the surface and uses words that address the underlying needs. Many clinicians (perhaps Freud being the first) have used icebergs to illustrate this important distinction between what's visible and what's happening on a deeper level. This is essential to the ALP model. Instead of butting

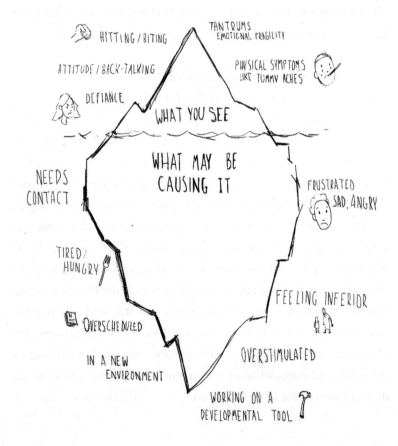

heads over the behaviors at the tip of the iceberg, you address them from the bottom up. Now you're connected, and your words are more effective.

Looking beneath the surface means translating kids' behaviors that may be annoying, off-putting, or even infuriating, and being the grown-up, or, in other words, the one who has the insight to see what's really happening. This is an important part of ALP that takes curiosity, "leaning in," and thinking to yourself, *What is he really telling me right now? What is underneath?* You may not always know, but if you practice seeing through this lens, you'll notice you feel more peaceful and effective in what you do and say next.

Using the ALP approach, you will begin to see that behind most irksome behaviors is a kid who is simply trying to learn the skills he needs to navigate the world.

Premise #3:
Big Emotions Are Like Storms

Now that you're using the iceberg analogy, you see that difficult behavior is not something to squash or sweep under the rug; it's an opportunity. Tantrums, not listening, hitting, and more are all overt signs that your child is working on a developmental skill and that he needs your understanding and guidance, not your worry, punishments, or anger.

If you see difficult moments this way, you can be a calm and steady navigator for your child. Emotions are like waves, and life is like being on the water—emotions are always there (otherwise life would be boring!). There are calm, rolling waters and there are storms that arrive and pass. In the boat, you're together and you ride the waves. If you stay calm and present, you can navigate, and know that the storms (intensely strong emotions) are a normal fact of being on the water, and they always pass. You don't have to yell or punish, nor do you have to cave or be indulgent.

Emotions are okay. They come and go, they aren't forever or scary. I'm here with you no matter what and I'm okay with all your feelings.

This isn't such a tall order when our kids are being easy. The challenge is when things get tense, messy, and emotional. In these moments, being open, patient, and communicating clearly can feel impossible. In fact, adult relationships are like this too. When things are going smoothly, we feel connected, but when one person does something we don't like, we don't agree with, or we don't understand, we tend to fight with them or freeze them out.

What psychologists know, through decades of research and clinical experience, is that if we keep communication open in tough times, it deepens our relationships. Children who are met with understanding and guidance in their most vulnerable moments have greater levels of self-regulation and more positive outcomes in school and with peers. Relationships in which people listen to each other with less judgment (even during disagreements) are stronger and healthier over time. When your child has a difficult emotion, imagine it as a wave that rolls under you, rather than hitting you straight on. Let it be okay instead of than feeling you have to fix it.

Kids bring their trickiest, most intense, and irrational emotions to us for a reason: we are the safe, trusted place to work them out. Behaviors are outward signs of your child's internal world, and they show you what her bustling, growing brain is working on. With the guidance and phrases in this book, you'll notice how difficult moments show you when your child needs you to connect and guide her, rather than shame or punish her. And you too can use these moments as a chance to stretch and grow as a human being.

Looking at Our Knee-Jerk Reactions

In our groups and private practice, we hear countless stories of how parents respond to difficult moments. Here are some of the most common statements they make about their "knee-jerk" reactions:

I am quick to get angry.

I use a harsh tone when my child is not listening.

I lose control and spank or hit my child, then I feel terrible.

I use spanking as an intentional form of punishment.

I can't stand it when my child has a tantrum.

I'm exhausted and overwhelmed, so I end up caving on a limit.

I feel anxious when my child gets upset.

I want my child to feel good or be happy all the time.

I doubt myself and my parenting.

HARSHNESS, RIGIDITY, OR NO INTEREST IN UNDERSTANDING

Parents who discipline harshly often do not explain the reasons behind rules or collaborate with their kids. They do not tolerate disobedience or unwanted feelings. The parents we work with who fall into this category often fear that they're not doing their job right and they're going to have a "bad" kid. If you were talked to this way as a child, you might hear your own parent's voice in your head. These moms and dads admit to us that they often talk to their kids in a way that they would never talk to anyone else. They don't necessarily want to do it, but they can't figure out a way to stop.

Harsh discipline can work in the short term, but it backfires. Kids who feel judged, scared, or humiliated by their parents are more likely to either rebel and engage in power struggles or, conversely, repress their feelings, instincts, and opinions. If kids are controlled by fear and judgment, they aren't challenged to develop their own moral compass. They don't build an internal sense of good that carries them through the moments when no one is watching. When we yell or use fear, kids shut down, which makes it impossible for them to absorb the nuances of all the life lessons parents need to teach. There's a shaming, critical stance on the part of the parent that, deep down, can give children the feeling that they're only loved when they're behaving well, rather than loved unconditionally. This is why harsh discipline undermines the greater parenting goals we identified on pages 2–3.

It's helpful to see the responses in this list as veering from too reactive or harsh to too indulgent or permissive. Most parents have moments of acting in one of these ways. Sometimes we swing from one to the other—trying to please and accommodate so much that we feel walked all over, get frustrated, snap, and swing to the other extreme.

PERMISSIVENESS, FLIP-FLOPPING, OR HELICOPTERING

On the other hand, there's the tendency for permissiveness and flip-flopping. To some degree, we all feel the urge to protect our little ones from suffering or struggle—sometimes we feel like our job is to keep our kids happy at all times. When they're frustrated, we swoop in and do their task for them; when they have a tantrum we get insecure and relax the limit we've set. Or we just want to be liked by our kids, so we have a hard time enforcing the rules and limits that make them mad. Parents with a permissive style often do not hold age-appropriate expectations for their children. They may not expect their kids to dress themselves or clean up after themselves at a reasonable age, or they may not hold a standard of social etiquette or social rules. They do not have reasonable maturity demands of their kids.

The paradox of permissiveness is that even though these parents are trying to make their kids happy, children often end up being less happy, less competent, less self-reliant, and more anxious. Their world is too undefined, and without consistent, reasonable boundaries, they don't feel completely safe. In our experience, it's also permissive parents who snap and explode out of nowhere because their frustration builds up. This can be scary and unexpected to both parents and kids.

We meet a lot of parents who know that you're not supposed to yell or spank. But they often feel frustrated and ineffective as they try so hard to be "nice," while their kids ignore them.

ALP allows you to be emotionally responsive while also being in charge and having clear expectations. You can listen and empathize with your child without going back on important limits, caving, or placating.

What Our Everyday Words Communicate

Everyday words and tone communicate a lot. Certain messages are overt and others are subtle. Let's look at some of the most common phrases parents use in difficult moments. You'll see yourself in some of these and not others (as moms, we do too!). Don't worry if you've said any or all of these statements—you don't have to censor or judge every word that comes out of your mouth. And if you do say something that later makes you cringe (as literally every parent in the world has), read "Repair and Circle Back" (page 52), because this process can bring you closer to your child again. We're listing all these common reactions for just that reason—they are common!

When our kids are having a hard time, we often have responses that are:

Judgmental and shaming

> *Stop whining. You should know better.*

> *How many times have I told you not to run away from me? Why would you do that? What's wrong with you?*

> *Be a big boy. Stop crying like a baby.*

Dismissive

> *Oh, it's not such a big deal, don't worry about that.*

> *Walk it off. You're okay.*

> *Let's think about something else.*

> *No, you're great at basketball, don't worry!*

Harsh

> *You're being terrible right now! I've had it.*

> *You're driving me up the wall. How many times do I have to tell you?*

Trying to cut off the communication

> *No. Just stop. Because I said so.*

> *No means no.*

Bribing

> *If you eat your vegetables, you can have dessert.*

> *If you get an A I'll give you five dollars.*

> *If you don't hit your brother all day today, you'll get a toy.*

Threatening and punishing

> *Do you want to go to time-out?*

> *You're not moving? Okay, see you later, bye-bye, I'm going to leave, then.*

> *If you do that again, you'll be sorry.*

Comparing

> *See how good Johnny is being? Look at him just sitting there nicely.*

Caving or flip-flopping

> *All right, never mind what I said before, watch more TV.*

> *Oh fine, stay up past your bedtime even though it's a school night.*

> *Five minutes more. Okay now I mean it. Okay now, five minutes more . . .*

Overhelping, helicoptering, or hovering

> *Here, let me do that for you. What's wrong? Let me fix it.*

A lot of these reactions are about making feelings go away, or controlling kids with fear. Threats and punishments translate to "I am using my power over you. I'm worrying or scaring you into doing something." The takeaway message is something like "I have to make you suffer or deprive you so you'll learn to do the right thing. You deserve something bad to happen for what you did." Punishments shut down problem-solving skills and do not support kids in practicing what *to* do. Bribing communicates, "You will only do the right thing if I trick you or bait you to do it. Once the bait is gone, you may not have learned anything and may not do the right thing the next time." Bribing can surely get you through stuck moments, but it can also work against you in the long run. We'll show you how to use natural consequences, enticement, and information to engage cooperation instead.

DO KIDS LEARN THROUGH REWARDS AND PUNISHMENTS?

Rewards and punishments can change a child's behavior in the short term, but the long-term outcomes are exactly the opposite of what most parents desire. Generally speaking, research shows that rewards lower intrinsic (internal) motivation and send the message that what you're trying to teach must be distasteful. Over time, the rewarded behavior fades because the child doesn't have any true connection to it—they've been performing for external validation. Punishments and harsh parenting tactics are, not surprisingly, associated with angry, aggressive behavior in children. Punishments are shaming and activate the fight or flight centers of the brain, which in turn shuts down the problem-solving and creative-thinking areas of the brain. Now your child is not able to learn the nuances of what you're trying to teach or come up with good solutions. So what does work? The best learning happens in the context of positive emotional interactions—this is a central finding of pioneer researcher Stanley Greenspan. Do you have a fond memory of a favorite teacher? When you think back on it, you might realize that not only did you have good feelings and interactions with this person, you also learned a lot more.

Confusing, overhelping, and helicoptering messages also miss the mark. We want our kids to develop resilience, and if we try to shield them from all hardship and struggle, they don't have the chance to learn or develop tolerance for tough feelings. If we swoop in and make our kids' suffering go away or take it on for ourselves, it tells them we can't handle it, and that we think they can't handle it either. Over time, kids get the message that only good feelings are acceptable.

If children are capable and built for good, none of these tactics are necessary. They all imply that a child needs to be tricked or forced to do the right thing. When we use them, it sends a message that we don't trust our kids and it keeps them from developing their internal sense of good. This also takes away a child's ability to find natural pleasure and enjoyment in life. The child instead acts for an external reward or evaluation from us.

In the next section, we'll give you a positive, accurate, and effective way to interact in everyday moments. The good news is that, since children are built with the capacity for empathy, connection, and cooperation, you can work *with* them rather than *against* them when you're moving through your day.

The Three Steps of ALP Communication: Attune, Limit Set, Problem Solve

This section will explain the basics of ALP communication. In the following chapters you will see how to apply it. Assuming no one is in danger, the first step is to watch, listen, and understand, or *attune*. The second step is to set and hold reasonable limits or state a reality. The third step is to engage your child in problem solving.

1. **Attune:** watch, listen, and understand

2. **Limit set:** state and hold reasonable limits or state a reality

3. **Problem solve:** engage your child in creating solutions

Not every situation calls for all three steps, and sometimes they happen out of order. The more you practice, the more you will personalize the language. To get a sense of what ALP looks like in a simple situation, read this scene. You'll see the dad respond to a tricky moment in two ways that fall into the categories of knee-jerk reactions described in the previous section. In the third response, he employs ALP.

Three-year-old Emily is in a toy store with her dad. She's engrossed in playing with a train table. Eventually, it's time to leave the store and Emily is not happy. She's mad and frustrated and starts to cry in protest. She is quickly escalating into a full-scale tantrum.

Response 1

Emily, why are you so upset? Don't cry! Okay, I know you love it here. We can stay. I'll call Mom and tell her we'll be late.

Response 2

Emily, stop crying right now and get over here. I said it was time to go and we're going. It's not a big deal. You're

acting like a baby and you better listen. Do you want to go to time-out?

Response 3

Emily, I know you're frustrated and don't want to go. It's really hard to leave such a fun place. We do have to go now; we're meeting Mommy in fifteen minutes. You can take my hand and we'll walk together and sing our silly song, or I'll gently pick you up and carry you out.

SAFETY FIRST

Sometimes the situation calls for a safety step. Block a child's foot from kicking another child, wrap your arms firmly around a child running into the street, or get down on the level of two toddlers taking swipes at each other while moving them apart. In moments of possible danger or harm, safety is the first priority before moving on to ALP.

Step 1: Attune

Attunement: Becoming aware of and receptive to another person's perspective. Communicating to the other person that you understand what he or she wants or is feeling.

Why is attuning to children so important? Well, answer the following two questions. We've asked them to hundreds of parents over the years and the responses have been consistent. *Cover the common answers below and write down your own before you look!*

1. When you are sad, mad, scared, frustrated, or upset, what do you want most from the person closest to you?

_____

_____

☐ empathy
☐ to have my feelings acknowledged and validated
☐ to be asked to talk more about it
☐ to be understood, even if the person doesn't agree
☐ to be taken seriously
☐ to be listened to without judgment

2. When you're sad, mad, scared, frustrated, or upset, what do you *not* like getting from the person closest to you?

_____

_____

☐ to be told my feelings are wrong
☐ when the first response is a "just fix it" solution
☐ to be ignored or for the person to shift to talking about him- or -herself
☐ to be pacified or patronized ("don't worry about it!")
☐ to be judged for how I feel
☐ to have my feelings dismissed or discounted

You can probably see where we're going with this. Whether you're a toddler melting down over the wrong pair of socks or a grown-up feeling rejected by a colleague at work, at the end of the day, we all yearn for connection. We want our trusted people to see and understand us, especially in vulnerable moments. We want to be heard, even when our feelings don't make sense or seem irrational to the other person.

Imagine that you express a tough emotion and your favorite person snaps at you, dismisses your feelings, or overreacts. You are left alone with your emotions and will either push them back inside, act out, or scream louder. You will learn that your feelings are not welcome or acceptable, or that you shouldn't express them because they'll make the other person upset. We wouldn't want to be talked to this way, yet we talk to our kids this way—whether it's because we can't see past their "bad" behavior, we see their problems (the wrong socks!) as insignificant, or we can't tolerate their feelings.

Now imagine how different it would feel if your trusted person paused, looked at you, nodded, and said, *I get it. That sounds hard. Tell me more.* You'd feel a little relieved. The pressure would be let out. The urgency of the emotion would be lessened, even if just a bit, and you wouldn't feel alone.

Babies and little kids need high levels of empathy from us, even when their reactions and behaviors seem irrational or bad. As parents, it's challenging to be empathic when we're frustrated and our kids are being difficult. This is the moment when we can snap, threaten, punish, or cave. But these hard moments are the ones when our kids need us the most. These are the times that will deeply shape their sense of self-worth and serve as a model of compassion for themselves and others.

If we want caring, confident, and resilient kids who feel safe expressing *all* their feelings to us and come to us when they need help (now, and when they're older), the first step in handling difficult moments is to attune.

IS THAT PERMISSIVE AND WORDY?

Some parents worry they'll have to do a whole lot of talking or come across as permissive. A dad once said to us, "You want me to attune to a four-year-old who has just broken the jar of spaghetti sauce I explicitly told him not to touch?" The answer is, yes. But it's important to know that attuning is not permissive parenting. Attuning to your child is not:

- Being lenient
- Making him happy all the time
- Preventing her from struggling or making mistakes
- Hovering or micromanaging
- Overtalking or overnegotiating

Attuning is:

- Pausing rather than reacting with your own feelings first
- Listening and watching with genuine curiosity
- Communicating that you understand or you're trying to understand
- Creating the experience of feeling seen and heard

Feelings Need a Place to Go

Feelings have to go somewhere. Clinicians who work with kids in therapy see that, over time, if feelings are ignored, judged, punished, or pacified, those feelings will eventually become either *internalized* (leading to symptoms like tummy aches, anxiety, poor self-image, trouble sleeping, and so forth) or *externalized* (leading to acting-out behaviors like hitting, biting, defiance, and tantrums).

INTERNALIZED	EXTERNALIZED
Tummy aches	Hitting
Anxiety/depression	Biting
Poor self-image	Defiance
Trouble sleeping	Tantrums

WHAT DOES IT MEAN WHEN A CHILD IS "ACTING OUT"?

In therapy, often parents will say that the child's teacher reports "acting out" behaviors. This might be defiance, hitting, disrupting the class, and so forth, but why exactly is it called acting out? It's because the child is having feelings and, rather than expressing them verbally, he or she is *acting them out.* The goal for a child like this (and for all children) is to help them verbalize their feelings. When they express themselves directly, the feelings don't need to be acted out, and adults can help.

When you attune, you offer a place for your child's feelings to go. As you listen and watch with genuine curiosity, you are able to avoid rushing to fix a problem, cutting your child off, or sending the message that certain feelings are not acceptable.

If you lead with understanding, you sidestep power struggles and work with your child, rather than against her. Taking the role of coach and helper to your child relieves your anxiety that you must control her at all moments, or make sure she's always happy.

I'm with you. I'm here to guide and help you. We're in this together.

Attuning also lowers your child's stress level and makes him more receptive to taking in information or learning the rule or behavior you want to teach, rather than feeling shamed or reprimanded. Attuning helps *you* feel less stressed, because you can see the problem from his perspective and reconceptualize it.

Communicating this way helps kids become emotionally intelligent, starting from babyhood. If children hear feeling words from a young age, the words come easily to them when they're older. Letting little ones know that all of their feelings are fine or interesting to you (not all of their behavior but, yes, all of their feelings) helps them to embrace and integrate those very normal and natural feelings we all have into their sense of who they are. Empathy comes from being empathized with. When kids get the sense of "feeling felt" it opens up their curiosity about what others are feeling too. Babies and kids who are responded to with empathy have a sense that the world is a good, safe place. This is the basis for secure attachment. They know that they are loved and of equal value, no matter how hard a time they're having, and they will, in time, be able to love and value others in their difficult moments. These emotional skills lead to resilience, because kids learn to weather life's bumps and get back on track.

Every time you attune rather than snapping, reacting with anger, jumping to set a limit, or giving in or cajoling to make your child immediately happy, it's like putting money in the bank. Over time, this thoughtfulness will pay off.

These are examples of attuned responses. When you read them, you might think, "But then my child won't know the rule," or "Then I'm caving or being permissive." Don't worry, this is just the first step. In some of these scenarios, you'll need your limit-setting and problem-solving steps too. We'll get to those steps in a few pages.

ATTUNE: LET YOUR CHILD KNOW THAT YOU UNDERSTAND

Listen and watch	Make eye contact and nod
Pause	Say what you see, or "sportscast"
Acknowledge	Paraphrase, or "the good waiter"
Look beneath the surface	Use feelings words
Bend or squat down	Be receptive and nonjudgmental
Say, "Tell me more"	Give space if needed

SCENARIO	AUTOMATIC RESPONSE	ATTUNED RESPONSE
Your toddler trips and falls.	You say, "Oh no!" and swoop her up. (Or) You tell her, "You're okay," without checking in with her.	You pause and watch. She looks back at you. You say, "I saw that. You okay?"
Your child doesn't want to leave the park.	I told you we have to go now!	Leaving while you're having fun is hard. You wish you could swing until it's nighttime!
Your baby pulls your hair.	No pulling hair. Bad!	You like to touch my hair, don't you?
Your baby resists a diaper change.	Hold still and stop wiggling!	You don't want to be doing this right now, I get it!
Your child doesn't want to wear his bike helmet.	Not up for discussion; you gotta wear it.	I know you don't want to wear it. It's not so comfortable, is it?
Your baby cries when you walk away from him.	Oh, you're okay! I'm only going to the bathroom!	I hear you. You don't want me to walk away from you.
Your toddler wants something from the grocery store.	No, I told you I'm not buying those cookies!	You want those cookies, huh? I know, they look good.
Your preschooler tells you a friend was mean to her.	That's not nice! Well, what did you say back? Did you tell a teacher? Don't play with her anymore!	I can see that didn't feel good. Tell me more about what was going on.
Your toddler says she's nervous about climbing a tricky ladder on the playground.	Don't be scared. It's easy.	I'm watching. You're wondering where to put your feet, huh?
Your child's ice cream cone falls on the ground.	You're okay, it's not a big deal. (Or) Oh no! Didn't I tell you to be careful?	Oh, man, I saw what happened there. You're feeling sad. I can see why!

As you can see in the examples, attuning is sometimes just a simple acknowledgment of what's in front of you. Still, you'd be amazed at how often parents forget this step (and sometimes, we do too!).

How to Attune

Attuning is personal; there isn't one right way. The words you choose, your body language, your tone of voice, and so forth will be different from the next person's. We are giving you a starting point to grow your own special ways to communicate attunement.

You can attune at any time—to happy, sad, angry, joyful, and silly moments. It's a way of engaging and it comes very naturally to certain people and less so to others. In this book, we focus on difficult moments because they're the ones when attuning is, well . . . difficult.

You'll inevitably catch yourself skipping the attune step sometimes, and that's okay. Habits are strong and you can always circle back for a "do-over." The more you practice, the more you'll incorporate attunement into daily interactions and see the benefits. You might even throw your child off guard a little by attuning when she expects you to immediately disagree!

It helps to keep a few phrases "in your back pocket," for times when you can't think of what to say. For example, "I hear you," "I get it," "ahh, I see . . ."

In this section, we'll give you tools for how to attune.

BUT I'M IN A BUSY GROCERY STORE!

How you respond depends on where you are. If you're in a public place, you have two other children to attend to, or you need to leave the house immediately, your attune step will look different. In the case of a grocery store or restaurant meltdown, you will kindly but confidently guide your child to a quiet spot to calm down. ALP is adaptable, as you will see from the scripts and conversations at the end of each chapter.

Pause

One of the best ways to practice the attune step is to pause before reacting. This is harder than it sounds—many of us have a habit of jumping in right away to react, snap, cut our child off, soothe, or fix a problem. Unless someone is in danger, practice not saying anything immediately. Or you can say something like,

Oh, uh-huh . . .

I see . . .

Hm, okay. . . .

Let's think about this . . .

Take a second to consider without rushing to stop, label, or solve. Time is your friend. This is your chance to glean what is happening with your child in this moment.

Use Your Body Language

The words you say are only a small part of communication. How your message comes across and the effect it has on your child is largely expressed in your body language and tone of voice.

You know this from personal experience. Imagine you're upset and your partner turns his or her back, or goes rigid and looks at you like you're crazy or annoying. It almost doesn't matter what words come out of his or her mouth, because body language "speaks" volumes. You're less likely to feel accepted or safe. Attunement and understanding, versus judgment and scorn, are conveyed powerfully by body language—the question is whether or not we are aware of what our bodies are saying.

WORDS ARE ONLY ONE WAY TO COMMUNICATE

Our ancestors evolved without the ability to speak words. Before the relatively recent development of speech, throat sounds and body language were likely how humans communicated important information to each other. Our brains are deeply programmed to respond to body language. Research tells us that the emotional content of a message is communicated almost entirely through nonverbal signals.

To convey that you're "on the same side" as your child, that you're not a threat, and that you're trying to understand, face her, make eye contact if you can, or put your hand on her shoulder, and get on her level.

Standing over your child is an offensive move.

At eye level is a collaborative move.

Relax your body, relax your face, open your stance, take your hands off your hips.

Many clinicians describe this body position as a way to signal safety. It keeps children from shutting down or pushing back. We especially like Tina Bryson and Dan Siegel's technique of getting yourself *below* your child's eye level if you can. This gives you more success at changing the power dynamic so your little one feels open.

Say What You See: The "Sportscaster"

Imagine you're a sportscaster and your job is to narrate in a factual, nonjudgmental way. We love to see parents using the sportscaster technique in all kinds of difficult situations. It helps kids stay open to hearing information, rather than feeling blamed and becoming defensive. It also helps them connect cause and effect. The key to the sportscaster is to keep your tone observant and curious, not shaming. Describe what you hear and see. For example,

You grabbed the blocks and your friend looks confused.

You're talking loudly and you can't hear the information I'm giving you.

I saw she took the toy from your hands.

Oh, man, the tower fell over.

Paraphrase: The "Good Waiter"

In your own words, say back to your child what she's told you. This is a great way to let her know you're curious and not necessarily trying to convince her out of her point of view.

> *So you're saying it's hard that other kids have chips and cookies in their lunch and you only have a sandwich and vegetables? You feel left out.*

> *It feels like you'll never get to go to the movies. It feels so far away you can't stand to wait.*

Imagine you're a waiter in a restaurant and you're making sure you got the order right. "You really want the pink Barbie towel." "You don't want your broccoli to touch your chicken!" "You want that toy Charlie is playing with!" The "good waiter" technique makes children feel understood: "So let me repeat your order to make sure I got it right. You want the pink Barbie towel, with broccoli on the side, and your special toy in a doggie bag." Ask your kids if you got it right, or if you're missing anything.

Parents sometimes tell us that they worry this will make it worse, but often it's more like deflating a balloon before it pops.

EXAMPLE: SAYING GOOD-BYE THE OLD WAY

Child: *I want to go with you! Waaaaa!!!!*

Dad: *I have to go to work! You're okay. Aw, stop crying!*

The toddler's cries get even louder and more insistent. Eventually, he has to be pried away from Dad.

SAYING GOOD-BYE THE GOOD WAITER WAY

Child: *I want to go with you! Waaaaa!!!!*

Dad (crouching down): *You really want me to take you along! I get it. It's hard to say good-bye.*

The child's cries quiet a bit and his eyes open wider. It's not an immediate fix, but by attuning, the emotional message becomes less urgent and demanding. (See how dad adds the limit-setting and problem-solving steps on page 49.)

It's amazing what happens when we let our kids tell us their thoughts and feelings without judgment or solutions right away. See for yourself how they react when you repeat back what your kids tell you, in your own words. They keep talking! Imagine how important that will be when they grow into teenagers.

Agree and Align

Don't be afraid to agree with your child if you do. The limit might remain, but that doesn't mean you can't join in with the feelings if yours are similar.

I wish we could see Batman on opening night too! Man that would be fun.

Use your Iceberg Analogy

Look at the behaviors at the tip of the iceberg on page 10 and practice seeing what's beneath the surface. This will help you be more patient, understanding, and empathic toward your child, and it will also give you more ideas for how to attune and also how to solve the problem. With your iceberg analogy, you may see that you have a sleep-deprived toddler, one who needs physical or emotional contact, or one who needs practice being in a group. When you see it this way, it helps you make attuned statements that connect below the surface.

I know, it's been a long day, I bet you're tired.

It's different here, isn't it? You're getting used to being with all these people.

It's easy to assume we know what's going on in a difficult moment, but don't assume. Gather more information.

Tell me more about this.

Help me understand what's making you upset.

Put yourself in your child's place and try to uncover it like a mystery. You don't know what it felt like, so let him tell you. If your baby is not yet verbal, say what you think he is feeling and why. If you don't know why, you can say, "I can tell you're upset but I'm not sure why yet."

PAUSING TO BE CURIOUS

Wendy learned ALP and was getting good at saying back what she thought her four-year-old son was feeling. One day, he got really upset at having to leave a party. She was in a hurry, so she quickly reflected, "I know it's hard to leave the party." But he kept on wailing. "I know, you don't want to leave," she said. But he seemed even more upset. Reflecting "wasn't working." Finally Wendy stopped, knelt down next to him, and gathered more information, "What are you trying to tell me?" Her son sniffled. "Tommy promised to show me his goldfish before I go, but now he's playing with someone else!" Ah, now she had taken the time to find out exactly what her son was upset about and she could attune in a much more specific and genuine way. "I understand now; you were expecting to see the goldfish and now you're worried you won't get to."

Remember that your child's brain doesn't work exactly the same way yours does. Little kids (depending on their age and temperament) naturally have lower tolerance for frustration, less flexibility, and fewer problem-solving skills. What seems obvious and important to you may not to him, and vice versa. Try not to insert or project your own feelings, but see his behavior as understandable, given his developmental level.

LABELING AND COMPLAINING ABOUT YOUR KIDS

Have you ever noticed how often people talk negatively about their kids while they're standing right there—we see this all the time! It's amazing how often parents think their kids aren't listening, or aren't capable of understanding (even babies understand), and talk about them as if they're not in the same room.

We know, it's comic relief and it's a joining moment when you can share with friends the parts of parenting that drive you insane. But labeling and complaining about your kids while they're with you compounds the problem ("Well, Daddy sees me this way; I must be this way."). All those challenging aspects of your kids' behavior can actually be seen as strengths—it depends a lot on your perspective.

Instead of, *Oh, she's being a nightmare. She's so difficult. She's killing me right now.*

Say, *She really knows what she wants. She's persistent and strong. She expresses her feelings really well, I definitely know when she needs me!*

Instead of, *Oh, he's shy. He has trouble when he meets people.*

Say, *He's thoughtful and he's always watching. He really thinks before he leaps, which I appreciate. He's soaking everything in; he respects boundaries; he likes to have time to warm up when he first meets people, which makes sense!*

Model Attuning to Others and Yourself

The most powerful way for your kids to "catch" this contagious way of being is to model it. Attunement can be applied in all your relationships. Your relationship with your partner is one of the best ways for your kids to absorb this empathic way of being. They are like little sponges and notice everything we do. We've had many parents say that practicing an empathic response with each other in difficult moments has improved their relationship significantly. Attune to yourself too and let your child know how you're feeling. "I am getting frustrated." "I got mad at myself when I forgot to . . ." "That really surprised me!" "I'm confused about this." "I'm not sure what to do."

Take baby steps by attuning to strangers. A mom told us a great story about how this made all the difference. She was a high-powered executive who had a quick temper. One day, she was jogging with her baby stroller and had music playing from a small speaker. The man next to her complained about the noise, which normally would have made her say something like "@#$!, I'm running, here!" or "Move if you have a problem with it!" Instead, this time, she made an attuned statement. "I understand, it must be bothering you," she said. "I'll hang back a bit and you can run ahead." The runner nodded and thanked her and, to her absolute shock, her own anger dissolved. She couldn't believe it. Attuning was almost like a magic pill that made the frustration go away. Practicing ALP this way helped her apply it with her baby.

Step 2: Limit Set

As parents, we help our kids learn social rules and etiquette, as well as family rules that are uniquely ours. We keep our kids healthy and safe, we keep the day moving on schedule, and often we're the ones to break the news to our kids that their desires and whims cannot always be satisfied. In other words, every day, we have to set limits.

Limits are a good thing. When there are clear, reasonable limits and rules, over time children get the feeling that the world makes sense and is a safe, reliable place. There's a grown-up in charge and they are free to be children, to play, explore, and test the world.

The limit-setting step is the moment when you state a boundary or rule and briefly explain the reason. It doesn't negate your child's feelings, it presents him with information. For example,

Hitting your brother is absolutely not okay. It hurts.

Phones are for big people. My phone is important for my work so I'm going to keep it.

The iPad does not belong at the table while we're eating.

Today is a looking day, not a buying day.

Use gentle hands with the dog, so we don't hurt her.

In this step, sometimes we state realities for kids, rather than a limit: a fallen ice cream cone, a helium balloon that got away, or the actions of others and circumstances we can't control. These are times when life just deals us realities that make us unhappy. For example,

The balloon floated away and we can't get it back.

We can't control what other people do.

You didn't get chosen for the team.

The toy store is closed and we can't go in.

It's raining, so we can't go play soccer.

These are the parts of life that just are, the parts we don't have choices about. We can have our feelings, and we can problem solve for solutions, but the limits and realities are what one of our school-age clients described as "It is what it is."

Here are some of our earlier examples, adding the limit-setting step.

SCENARIO	ATTUNE	LIMIT SET
Your child doesn't want to leave the park.	Leaving while you're having fun is hard. You wish you could swing until it's nighttime!	We have to go now, because it's almost dark and time to make dinner.
Your baby pulls your hair.	You like to touch my hair, don't you?	It's not okay to pull hair because that hurts.
Your baby resists a diaper change.	You don't want to be doing this right now, I get it!	I have to change you now because your diaper is wet.
Your child doesn't want to wear his bike helmet.	I know you don't want to wear it. It's not so comfortable, is it?	The rule in our family is that you do have to wear it to keep you safe.
Your baby cries when you walk away from him.	I hear you. You don't want me to walk away from you.	I have to go because I have a meeting this morning.
Your toddler wants something from the grocery store.	You want those cookies, huh? I know, they look good.	We're not buying that today because we're just getting what we need for our meals.

Beyond "Because I Said So!"

Why not just yell or tell your kids, "Do what I say and that's it"? It may feel like the easiest route in the moment, but in the long run, we're here to help them develop a sense of right and wrong—one they carry into the world. We don't want our kids to follow rules or do what we say out of fear, or because there's a consequence. We also don't want them to grow up doing what other people say without question. Adding information with your limit is a respectful way to communicate—it implies that you see your child as a person worthy of understanding the background.

We use quiet voices in the library, because other people here are reading books.

Children value reasoning just as much as adults do, and explanations help bring awareness to future scenarios. It all seems so obvious to us and it's easy to get impatient when we need to repeat or explain. But most of us would agree that we want our kids to respect other people's opinions, thoughts, and feelings—and this starts with us doing the same and including them in our "behind-the-scenes" reasoning.

INSTEAD OF "NO"

You might feel tempted to say "no" when your baby or child tries to pull apart the pages of a book, splashes in the dog's water bowl, or hits a friend. This impulse is understandable, but there's a better way to start. There are lots of reasons for you to replace "no" with other limit-setting words. Here are some of those reasons—we're sure you could come up with more reasons on your own.

THE WORD "NO" . . .

- Doesn't contain details or an explanation.
- Ends the conversation, when your goal is to keep communication open.
- Loses its usefulness when it's heard all the time.
- Will surely be said back to you if you say it over and over.
- Can feel shaming or scary.

This doesn't mean you accept behaviors that are not okay, or that you shouldn't be 100 percent consistent about teaching respect for boundaries, not hurting people's bodies, social etiquette, and so forth.

Instead, offer a short, informational sentence. For example: "Gentle when you touch the dog," or "Please don't touch; the glass is delicate," or "It's not okay to pull my hair, because that hurts." If safety is an issue—your child is running toward the street, edging toward the top of a staircase, or looks about to hit a friend and you need to quickly intervene—words like "Stop!" or "Freeze" can be more specific and helpful.

Don't Be Afraid of the Reaction

So many parents tell us they're *afraid* of their kids' reactions. A mom we worked with kept telling us, "Oh, she'll be too sad. She won't like it when I tell her this." She admitted that every time she had to tell her daughter something she wouldn't like, she worried about it and often bribed her daughter not to feel bad. She couldn't state simple realities and limits like "Your sister is going to a sleepover and dad and I are going out to dinner. The babysitter is taking care of you tonight." Or, "Your sister's friend is coming over, but not your friend today." She shied away from breaking what she saw as "bad news" to her daughter, because she was literally afraid of the daughter's angry or disappointed reaction. She was trying to avoid her daughter's natural disappointment, which led to her daughter being more in control of the situation, and Mom resorted to bribing.

How Much Oomph, and How Many Times?

If you have a sensitive, watchful, tuned-in child, then stating the limits in a mild, matter-of-fact tone is better, so you don't overwhelm or risk shaming him. However, if you have a very strong-willed, challenging child, you may need more oomph in your voice, so it's heard. A strong-willed child needs you to get his attention, and to know you're confident and strong in your limits; otherwise, those limits don't feel clear and containing.

If you find yourself wondering why you've had to set the same limit fifty times, you're doing good work, don't worry. While some kids only need to hear a limit once to internalize it, for others, the limit-setting step has to be repeated, very patiently and relentlessly, many, many times before they are done testing and are ready to trust that limit. This is where your consistency over time will pay off. As kids get older, if you have consistently held reasonable limits without caving or flip-flopping, they will internalize these lessons and their testing of them will naturally decrease.

Step 3: Problem Solve

Now it's time to get creative. The problem-solving step is when you help kids figure out a solution. You've attuned, you've stated the limit or reality of the situation, and now is the opportunity to solve the problem with ideas that come from one or both of you. If the issue is between two friends or siblings, then part of your problem-solving step will be to "scaffold" conflict resolution. You will read more about how to do this in the hitting and physical behaviors chapter, as well as the sibling chapter.

"Here's What You Can Do": Creating an Optimist

The gist of the problem-solving step is "Here's what you *can* do!" to fulfill your intention, solve your dilemma, or recover from your emotional overload. It ends on a positive, forward-moving note and lends to the overall atmosphere of empathy and nonjudgment.

An enormous benefit of modeling problem-solving skills in difficult moments is that your children will, over time, apply these skills in many areas of their lives. Cultivating problem-solving skills helps kids with academics and independent learning, relationships, and more. They learn to see the world from a broader, more open-ended and optimistic perspective and will take on one of the hallmarks of optimists: the sense of being in control of the situation. When things don't go their way, optimists feel a sense of agency to overcome, rather than the pessimist's tendency to blame outside forces for their problems.

The "Head-Scratching, Bumbling Parent"

Problem solving also taps into and cultivates creativity. There are many ways to solve a problem and, with little ones, it can be easy and fun to think outside the box and be imaginative and willing to experiment with some crazy ideas. For many kids, it helps them think creatively when you use what we call the "head-scratching, bumbling parent." "Hmm, what *could* we do here?" is your tone, as if you truly do not have all the answers and are genuinely looking for help moving forward. It's developmentally normal for kids to get bogged down in black-and-white thinking, and using this approach opens up their thinking to more possibilities.

Scratch your head (literally or figuratively) and wonder aloud what the solution or next step could be, rather than rushing to give choices or solve the problem yourself every time.

> *So, hmm, I hear you saying that you want to buy a smoothie. But, jeez, I remember last time we got one that size, you didn't drink it. (Pause). Let's think what would make sense here . . .*

After you've wondered aloud, wait and see what happens. If your child knows that you won't always swoop in with the solve, she feels like you're a team. You may still have to hold a limit (for example, you may decide the limit is that you're going to split a smoothie), but create a little space for her to come along on the decision process.

Use Humor or Say Something Unexpected

A great way to open your little one up to creative thinking is to give an absurd option, like boarding your imaginary spacecraft as a way to exit the park. It's not hard to go a little off the beaten path.

> *I'm feeling a silly song coming into my head . . . Here, I'll sing it to you while we brush your teeth.*

> *You can hold this cardboard box while I change your diaper.*

> *I'm going to stand on my head while I think about this.*

Collaborate on a few options for what to do, given the limit or reality. Sometimes your child will be the one to come up with the creative solution to the problem, and sometimes it will be you. You can test the waters with asking for input, but if your child isn't able to make a choice or offer a solution that keeps the limit intact, then you can take over and lay out one or two choices.

Use a "Follow-Through" Choice

In some cases, you will need to use a "follow-through" choice in the problem-solving step. The follow-through choice is like your parenting escape hatch—a plan for taking over and making something happen when it needs to happen now. The follow-through choice may be telling your child that he can get in the car seat himself or you're going to help him do so, saying your preschooler can come to the table herself or you will help her body to the table, or letting your child know he can put back the toy or you will do it for him. We don't want you to go straight to the follow-through choice unless time is short. In the chart below, you'll see that the first scenario has a follow-through.

SCENARIO	ATTUNE	LIMIT SET	PROBLEM SOLVE
Your child doesn't want to leave the park.	Leaving while you're having fun is hard. You wish you could swing until it's nighttime!	We have to go now, because it's almost dark and time to make dinner.	So, hmm, should we do "follow the leader" out? (Pause.) Seems like it's hard to leave. You can walk yourself or I will carry you (follow-through choice).
Your baby pulls your hair.	You like to touch my hair, don't you?	It's not okay to pull hair because that hurts.	Let me hold your hand and show you how to touch hair gently.

SCENARIO	ATTUNE	LIMIT SET	PROBLEM SOLVE
Your baby resists a diaper change.	You don't want to be doing this right now, I get it!	I have to change you now because your diaper is wet.	Ready to hear the silliest song in the whole wide world?
Your child doesn't want to wear his bike helmet.	I know you don't want to wear it. It's not so comfortable, is it?	The rule in our family is you do have to wear it to keep you safe.	You can pick out any helmet you want within our price range.
Your baby cries when you walk away from him.	I hear you. You don't want me to walk away from you.	I have to go because I have a meeting this morning.	I'll sing our good-bye song and kiss both cheeks like I always do.
Your toddler wants something from the grocery store.	You want those cookies, huh? I know, they look good.	We're not buying that today because we're just getting what we need for our meals.	Do you want to put it back or should I carry it like a baby back to the shelf?

Remember this example? Added to our "A" step, here are the "L" and "P" steps—attuning, limit setting, and problem solving all together:

EXAMPLE: SAYING GOOD-BYE THE OLD WAY

Child: *I want to go with you! Waaaaa!!!!*

Dad: *I have to go to work! You're okay. Aw, stop crying!*

The child's cries get even louder and more insistent. Eventually, he has to be pried away from Dad.

SAYING GOOD-BYE THE ALP WAY

Child: *I want to go with you! Waaaaa!!!!*

Dad (crouching down): *You really want me to take you along! I get it. It's hard to say good-bye. I have to go to work now, and you're off to school soon. What should we do if we miss each other today? You know what, I think I'm going to write a note to you. Would you do the same for me at school?*

Over time, the language of attunement and collaboration helps kids feel more open and less adversarial. Problem solving becomes easier as the months and years go on because your child trusts that you respect his intentions and feelings. You are definitely going to set limits on his behavior, while at the same time you're helping him create and choose an acceptable solution. You're not here to dictate and enforce unreasonably, and you do care about his intention and input.

Calm Down instead of Time-Out

The old-fashioned version of time-out is a punishment, and we do not recommend it. When kids misbehave, have a tantrum, or similar, these are signs that they need guidance, teaching, or understanding. Punishment is counterproductive. It does not teach children anything except to fear a consequence, and to know that if they step out of line, they will be isolated from their most trusted people. Isolating a child and sending her to her room or another place in the house can make her feel shamed and alone.

Rather than using a punishment form of time-out, use calm down. Calm down is for anyone who is feeling overwhelmed or is unable to follow family rules and needs a break. Calm down is not a punishment. It's meant to be helpful and should be talked about as such. When your child is having big feelings, has hit or hurt someone, cannot follow a family agreement, or needs to regroup for any reason, you can gently lead her to calm down, or she may choose to go there herself. There will be times when you need to pick your child up and take her to calm down, but the message you're sending is that you are helping. This shows unconditional love and acceptance, which is especially important to convey in difficult moments. Stay with her if your presence or physical contact helps her calm down. If she wants space, tell her you'll check on her in a minute and walk away. Decide together when she's ready to go back to what she was doing, or move to another problem-solving tool. In the chapters that follow, you'll see examples of how to use calm down if you're in a grocery store and need to move your child outside or you're at a friend's house and have to take your child into another room. Calm down can even happen as you're walking away from the scene.

Here's an example of how to use calm down instead of time-out.

A mom and her two kids are at the beach. One child is playing too roughly with his sister. She's saying, "Stop it!" and he's not listening to her. The sister starts to cry.

TIME-OUT

> **Mom:** *Hey, cut it out! Get over here! I've told you before to be nice to your sister! You're getting a time-out!*

In this scenario, Mom scolds her son and withholds her attention while the child sits in isolation. When the timer goes off, she forces him to say, "I'm sorry." He feels embarrassed and resentful towards his sister and his mom.

CALM DOWN

> **Mom:** *Whoa, okay I saw that. That was too rough. Come and sit with me for a few minutes to calm down. You're showing me you need a break to regroup. I'm going to help you take a breather.*

In this scenario, Mom sits with her son for a few minutes, checks in with him about whether he needs water or a snack, or if it's time to call it a day. After a bit, she says, "Do you feel ready to play again? Please check in with your sister and listen to what she wanted to tell you."

If you choose to make a calm-down space in the house, it can include items like these:

- Floor pillows
- Squeeze balls, yoga ball, and other tactile objects
- Loveys
- Tent or teepee
- Photo album of family members
- Music
- Notebook and writing/drawing materials

Repair and Circle Back

There will always be moments when we overreact, mishandle a situation, or say something we wish we could take back. This breakdown in communication—when our kids feel pushed away, punished, scared, or judged by us—is what clinicians call a "rupture." Some ruptures are benign and part of the ebb and flow of daily life, like having a moment of mild to moderate frustration when your child ignores you or you lose your patience and raise your voice. We can't always be perfectly in sync and it's normal (and even healthy) for these benign ruptures to happen between kids and parents. Other ruptures are what psychiatrist Dan Siegel describes in *Parenting from the Inside Out* as "toxic," and these are more disturbing to children; for example, screaming, hitting, insulting, or scaring a child. Over time, if these ruptures are not addressed, the child is left alone with feelings of shame and fear.

Ruptures need to be repaired. It's good to repair benign ruptures, and it's imperative to repair toxic ones. This also applies to fights between parents that happen in front of children. Repair is when we help our kids make sense of what happened. It brings us back together and kids get the sense that we're still "with" them, even if something difficult happened. Repair is part of how babies and children build trust—they see that even when people disagree and become disconnected, they come back together again.

Parents sometimes tell us they don't want to repair because it undermines their authority. Others don't repair because they feel guilty about what they've done, they think no one noticed, or they hope it'll be forgotten if it's not mentioned again. But memories don't work this way. Kids notice and register our words and reactions all the time. If they feel a rupture, they log it and it stays with them. If they can't make sense out of why it happened, the memory can be stored in a way that compromises their future relationships. It's like a piece of the puzzle is missing.

When you repair, you put a piece of the puzzle back into place.

This is an opportunity we don't want you to miss. It's not important or (even helpful) for you to be perfect, and owning your mistakes can be a humbling moment that levels the playing field in a good way. This is a chance to reinforce that you're not afraid to talk about tough moments and mistakes. Your children need you to model this in order to accept and embrace their own imperfect moments and mistakes throughout their lives. Being aware of moments when you lose it or react in a harsh or misattuned way is the first step. The next step, once you feel calm, is to go back and help your child make sense of those bumpy times. Be open to apologizing, owning your reactions, or just circling back to debrief. Say something like,

Remember what happened yesterday? I was really feeling frustrated, did you notice that? I used a loud voice and I got upset. I think I forgot to take some deep breaths. What I meant to say was . . .

Mom and I used loud voices with each other earlier today. I'm sure you could tell we were upset. We weren't understanding each other, and that happens even for grown-ups! We had to work at listening and coming up with a new plan.

Wow, I really used a mad voice just now and forgot to let you know I understand your idea. I am here to help figure this out. Let me try again.

I'm sorry I got frustrated and grabbed that toy from you in the store. Next time, I'll help you put it back yourself.

Even if you handled the moment as you wanted to, you can always ask questions or make observations.

Are you feeling better? What do you think happened there?

So, I took the train set and put it away, and that made you feel sad? Got it. Anything else I missed about what happened?

Is there anything you think we could do differently next time?

ALP is a practice that, over time, becomes your go-to habit. It might feel difficult; you will "mess up" sometimes and you won't get it perfect—that's okay, doing it perfectly is not the point. Parenting is made up of thousands of small moments that together tell a story that can be beautiful and meaningful. Don't worry too much about getting it right every time. In fact, you'll see that even messing up is an opportunity for good.

ALP Cheat Sheet

ATTUNE: Let your child know that you understand.

Listen and watch
Pause
Acknowledge
Look beneath the surface
Bend or squat down
Say, "Tell me more"
Make eye contact and nod
Say what you see, or "sportscast"
Paraphrase, or the "good waiter"
Use feelings words
Be receptive and nonjudgmental
Give space if needed

LIMIT SET: Tell your child how it really is and briefly say why.

Set the limit or state the reality
Be calm
Don't ask questions
State family rules
Be consistent
Explain briefly

PROBLEM SOLVE: Explore better choices, suggest ways your child can help solve the dilemma.

Create
Be positive
Give choices
Push the envelope
Collaborate
Use humor
Use your "bumbling parent"

Proactive Tools

TOOLS FOR THE FAMILY

TOOLS FOR KIDS

TOOLS FOR ADULTS

Remember from chapter 1 that emotions are like waves. Imagine you and your little cocaptain are in your boat together. Small, rolling waves of emotion move the boat throughout the day. Now imagine that, as the parent, you have the advantage of being able to read the water and see the bigger waves or storms ahead. Your experience and foresight (your parenting binoculars) allow you to plan ahead and see trouble spots on the horizon. You know the signs that you or your child is running low on energy, food, or sleep, and when transitions will be hard. This helps you plan ahead and anticipate difficult moments, rather than only reacting after they happen.

This chapter outlines important proactive tools. When you use them, you will notice that you have fewer stuck or overwhelmed moments, and that you can move through them more easily. There will always be struggles and meltdowns, and we don't want you to try to circumvent all of them. Flip your thinking from "I hope we have a good day today. No tantrums, okay?" to "We don't know what today will be like, but let's see. We're in it together!"

Tools for the Family

These are practices that will help the family as a whole.

Family Meetings

So often, when we work with families who are struggling with difficult behaviors or challenging moments with their kids, we'll ask them, "What's your family agreement about that kind of thing?" or "Have you talked about this at a family meeting?" Most of the time we get blank looks. Family meetings just aren't something many of us ever did or considered. But they are an effective, even essential practice.

Family meetings are a great way to help establish open lines of communication, as well as family expectations (see an example of family agreements in chapter 5, on page 194). The tone of family meetings is positive, can-do-together, rather than scolding or negative. In family meetings, all ideas are welcome. Listen to each person's input with your attune tools. You can start off family meetings with phrasings like these:

So, we have our weekend trip coming up. I have some information about that.

I wanted to talk about getting out the door in the morning for school. It still feels hard, and I wanted to see who has ideas.

How's everyone doing with the screen time agreements we set up? Should we look at them again, or are they working well?

Who has something they want to share or talk about?

It helps when the agenda for the meeting includes all kinds of family doings. If you make it about only problem and rules, everyone will come to dread it. Give everyone a chance to say something. Include kids in family meetings as young as possible. Your toddler might at first wander off, but over time, she'll see this as a regular practice that everyone takes part in, and (as long as it has a tone of togetherness) she'll eventually want to be involved. In family meetings, let everyone share ideas and bring up issues important to them. If your three-year-old's contribution is that she likes the new magnets on the refrigerator, or if she repeats a funny piece of dialogue from the latest Disney movie, thank her for her thoughts and move to the next person. If your older child wants to take notes, that's great. Look at all the ideas and circle the ones that work best, given the family agreements. Create an overall visual diagram of the meeting to refer back to.

We worked with a mom who told us family meetings turned into a "complainfest" that her school-age daughters would nag and whine through. We suggested turning their criticisms into direct wishes or ideas for the future. At the next meeting, when her daughters starting complaining, she said,

> *That sounds hard—you're saying she hurt your feelings. So, as you know, in family meetings we say what we do want, not what we don't want. Make a clear statement to your sister about what your idea or request is.*

Mom kept the meeting from turning negative by validating her daughters' feelings, while putting the focus on new ideas and problem solving. Within a few weeks, the daughters were able to use the family meetings to talk to each other productively.

Have a family meeting once a week, or at least once a month. Any family member can also call an unscheduled family meeting.

Couples Meetings

Kids feel less anxious and more contained when they know their parents are on the same page. Presenting a united front can make a big difference in decreasing kids' confusion and their inclination to test out potentially negative behaviors. Kids are less likely to play one parent against the other and parents are less likely to cave on a limit because they want to be the popular one. We've worked with all kinds of families on this idea: single parents, separated parents, multigenerational families, families with nannies, and so forth. One of the best gifts you can give to each other and your kids is to find common ground and have strategies you agree on and rules you stick to.

Talk about this book. Each of you doesn't have to use the exact same words, but the overall ALP approach can help you be consistent and predictable to your kids. Talk about problems, solutions, new family rules, changes in routines, or expectations with your partner first. This way, you can present new information to your kids together. If your partner isn't there and something important arises that you're not sure how to handle, let your kids know you'll discuss it and get back to them.

Of course, I have to check with Mom. We're a team.

Don't criticize your partner in front of your kids on a parenting issue. Make a note to discuss it in private later. The respect your partner will feel and the opportunity to work out disagreements privately can improve the cohesiveness and sense of peace in your family. It also gives both of you time for the big emotions to pass and for your more rational, helpful self to emerge.

Show affection. Being affectionate (in a nonsexual way) with your partner in front of your kids has positive effects, including increasing their sense of security and giving them an example of a healthy relationship. Make a habit of warm hugs and kisses at hello and good-bye, holding hands or a hand on the shoulder to show support or for no reason at all, and say, "I love you." A nod of the head, a smile, a look of "I get it, I know you" conveys a connection and our kids pick up on these small gestures. We tend to be more affectionate with our kids than we are with our partners. If we can share something we've learned in many years of parenting classes and couples therapy, parents miss and long for those simple shows of affection that they remember from their early days as a couple. These baby steps can bring a couple closer again.

Why and how to fight in front of your kids. Constructive arguing with your partner in front of your kids can have a positive effect, as long as your communication with each other is respectful and shows effective conflict resolution skills. If every time you disagree you say, "Not in front of the kids," your kids never have a model for how to work through a disagreement in a kind and empathic way. Modeling ALP with each other (partner to partner) in front of your kids is a powerful teaching tool. It lets them know that you can love someone while not always having the same ideas or getting along perfectly. Listen to each other and let the other know you understand (attune step); set your boundaries or state the reality (limit-setting step); and come up with a solution, compromise, or something to try next time (problem-solving step).

REPAIR WITH KIDS AFTER YOUR FIGHTS

If you have a fight in front of your kids, always repair with them (in addition to your partner) after you've had a moment to calm down, or in the midst of an argument if you're able to speak calmly and reassuringly. We cannot state enough the importance of this for children.

> *Mommy and I have different ideas here, as you can tell! We're trying to solve a problem together.*

> *Remember earlier today when Dad and I were arguing? We had big feelings and I know our voices must have been loud. Each of us had really different ideas and we got upset. Finally we did figure out how to hear each other, though.*

When you do this, you help your child make sense of what happened. A puzzle piece in her mind is put into place. If you don't help her make sense of what's happened, the story goes unresolved, or she draws conclusions in her mind that may not be accurate at all.

Tools for Kids

The Preparation Step

The preparation step is a helpful proactive tool for many different settings, and it's a small investment that can have a large payoff. Preparing for a new circumstance or change of environment and the expectations involved *before* it happens can make a big difference. You'll see the "prep step" used strategically in certain scripts throughout the book.

For example, if you know there's a trouble spot on the horizon, or if something has become a pattern, you will reap huge benefits by talking it out *before* it happens again.

> *Okay, we're going to be eating in a restaurant—on our way there can anyone tell me what rules we have in restaurants? We stay with our bottoms or knees in the chair—super. What else? Yes, we talk in an inside voice—good one! Who has another one?*

> *We're headed to the birthday party, and I had a thought. I remember last time when you felt really upset in the bouncy house because the kids were much bigger. What could we do this time—wanna give me a signal if it's getting too rough?*

> *Since we're going to the park and there will be other friends there, I'm reminding you that we use gentle touch when we're playing, and keep everyone's bodies safe.*

Think aloud with your kids during the preparation step:

(Parent bends down to talk to two kids at eye level): *You two are sitting next to each other, do you think that's going to work? Will you be able to focus, or is it going to be distracting for you?*

> *I see you starting to take the Legos out. I know it's hard to stop doing something in the middle of it when you're having fun. Dinner will be ready in ten minutes and then you'll need to pause, will that work?*

Getting out the door, having a diaper changed, shifting into bedtime routine, coming in and out of the car, coming to the dinner table, turning off the TV, leaving a friend's house—all of these transition moments are ripe for struggle and big feelings. Whenever possible, give your child a prep step. We prefer to phrase this in the positive, as in, "Do your last thing," or "Three-minute heads-up," rather than the more ominous-sounding, "Five-minute warning!"

We're heading out in five minutes—everyone do your last thing!

Five-minute heads-up.

Three more minutes until we shift into wind-down mode.

We're almost at school—does everyone know what to do when I park?

In two minutes, we're all going to start cleaning up.

Daddy's going to change your diaper in two minutes.

It may sound funny to give a baby a heads-up when she has no concept of time, but the point is to communicate respectfully and eventually children learn that we prepare them rather than just plucking them up. Over time, this helps them become an integrated part of the team.

Even when you use your most brilliantly timed preparation step, you may still need all your ALP steps, and that's okay. Refer to chapter 5 for ALP for listening and cooperation.

BAG OF TRICKS

Bring a bag of toys and interesting (and safe) nontoy items with you any time your baby or child might need them. Your bag of tricks can include novel toys, markers and paper, books, stickers, and so forth. Magnetic toys, figures, coloring books, and the like are especially good for travel and restaurants. Going to be in an airport? Buy a bouncy ball on an elastic string that attaches to the wrist.

FROM JULIE: BALLET BLANKET

From when he was three until he was six years old, I used to bring my son to my ballet class. He had a colorful blanket to sit on, and interesting toys and snacks. He would sit on the blanket and occasionally beckon to me between combinations. But he waited until the end of class to come off of his blanket. Then we would race back and forth across the classroom and the teacher would lift him high into the air. It was the sweetest thing, but it's almost certain that without the planning I did, he would not have been able to make it through the class. I loved that he was exposed to dance and live classical piano and had an opportunity to be a part of what I love.

The prep step can take place a day before.

I added some items to the calendar on the refrigerator. Can everyone come and take a look at what's on this week?

I've got the bath running. Everyone lay out your clothes and pack your backpacks for tomorrow before hopping in.

Checking in with you—are your ballet slippers where you need them for tomorrow?

You can start doing this with babies, because they absorb your intentions even when they don't understand every word. Planning the day before makes morning departures smoother. It's also considerate and kind to let your kids know what to expect rather than dragging and herding them around. Just like you would tell your partner or friend—rather than carrying them from place to place all day—talk to your kids and let them know what to expect.

We worked with the parents of a three-year-old girl named Maya who had very strong, loud opinions. Her mom and dad seemed terrified of her reactions and tiptoed around her, trying desperately to please her. In many ways, she was in charge instead of her parents. One of their biggest challenges was getting her dressed for school in the morning. No matter how many different outfits they offered her, Maya dug her heels in and wouldn't wear any of them. We'd been working with the parents on ALP and suggested they add a prep step, having her choose her clothes the night before. They came to the next session saying it didn't work. "What happened?" we asked. "Oh, she changed her mind again," the mom lamented. "Wait, sounds like you forgot the 'L' step," we commented. It was true; she needed her parents to hold the limit. When she melted down, they had to empathize, but not allow her to change her mind after the clothes had been chosen. It took her four mornings to trust they meant business. After that, she got in the rhythm of choosing clothes the night before and sticking with the choice, and dressing went much more smoothly.

Filling the Tank

When your kids are running low on their basic needs for sleep, healthy food, exercise, and downtime, they are more vulnerable to feeling stressed and acting out. Review the following needs to see if the family needs to refill.

Sleep. Improving sleep, on its own, can turn around what seems like a behavioral problem. When kids are sleep deprived, even by just thirty minutes per night, they are less capable of managing their emotions and more likely to have tantrums and other behavioral issues. When we sleep, information is transferred from short-term to long-term memory and learning is solidified. Well-rested people are more creative, flexible, and better able to solve problems. The issue we see every day in our practice is that kids do not tell us (with words) when they need more sleep, they need us to know their sleep needs and make sleep a priority. In fact, sleep-deprived kids often look wired and hyperactive, so it's easy to miss the signs they need an earlier bedtime. It's up to us as parents to protect this building block of health.

Toddlers need eleven to twelve hours of nighttime sleep, plus a nap. School-age children still need ten to twelve hours of nighttime sleep. If you believe your child is not getting enough sleep or his sleep habits are a struggle, it's a good idea to read our book *The Happy Sleeper* for specific strategies on improving bedtime, nighttime, and naptime sleep problems or refer to TheHappySleeper.com for individual help.

Food. When we don't eat well, low energy, shakiness, difficulty concentrating, and irritability hijack our frustration tolerance and emotional flexibility. As grown-ups, we can identify our own feelings of hunger and fix it immediately, but imagine if these feelings came over you and you had no idea why or how to make them go away—this is how little kids feel when they're hungry.

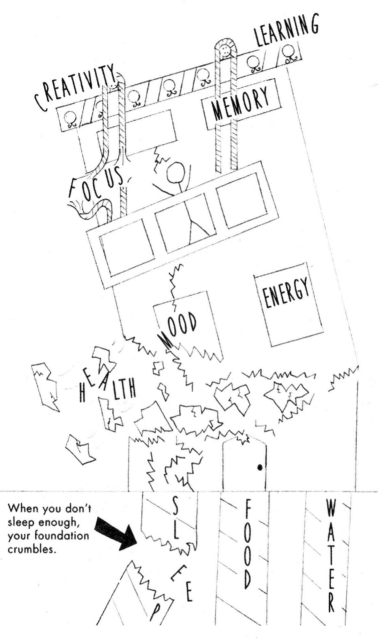

CREATIVITY
LEARNING
MEMORY
FOCUS
ENERGY
MOOD
HEALTH

When you don't sleep enough, your foundation crumbles.

SLEEP
FOOD
WATER

From *The Happy Sleeper*

Keep this in mind as you plan your day. Do you need snacks for the car at school pickup or ice water after soccer practice? Here are two tips when using the prep step for hunger:

- Make the snacks healthy and low in sugar (avoid juices and sweetened foods). Think mini versions of meals. Julie's mom would respond to the predinner "I'm so hungry" pleas by doling out carrot sticks to her four kids. Carrots have just enough natural sugar to quickly temper the grumpiness and buy a little time.
- Pay attention to the time. If it's been about three hours or more since the last meal or snack, hunger may be the cause of difficult behavior. Avoid offering food as a way to soothe, distract, or as a bribe, as this can lead to emotional eating.

Movement. Exercise has an immediate effect on a person's state of mind. Research suggests that even taking a brief walk increases creativity. When people exercise, they perform better on tests of executive function (organizing thoughts and making decisions), and over time, exercise promotes the creation of new brain cells in the hippocampus—an area of the brain important for learning and memory. We all have more focus, patience, and energy when we get up and move our bodies on a regular basis.

There are many ways to use movement proactively. Talk a walk while you problem solve, schedule movement breaks every fifteen minutes during homework, use standing desks at home, do jumping jacks or handstands when you know everyone's tank is almost empty, or dance to music while you clear the table. Find your family's best ways to keep moving.

Overscheduling. It's great to have piano lessons and playdates, but most of us can feel when it's too much. When kids are overscheduled, life becomes hectic, preplanned, and parent directed. They end up being led around by a grown-up all day: to school, child care, sports, errands, music, ballet, homework, chores, dinner, and bedtime. They don't feel in control of their lives. It doesn't leave breathing room to let moments unfold spontaneously, based on whatever idea comes up and whoever is around.

When too many life elements collide, kids are more likely to have emotional floods. The antidote to this is to protect unscheduled downtime and to use child-led play (page 76). Get rid of one after-school activity; have a screen-free, reading-only day on the weekend; take a destinationless walk in the neighborhood; lie in the grass and look at trees; clear out excess toys and put open journals and markers out on the coffee table; have a bubble bath after school—all of these will help.

As with sleep and hunger, kids can't necessarily identify that they're overscheduled, ask to slow down, or know how good it will feel, so you will need to guide them. Talk explicitly about your family's ways of finding balance.

We're taking a break from soccer this round, so we can keep open afternoons for just seeing what happens.

FILLING UP ON *YOU*

A friend and mom of three little kids shared some wisdom with us recently. She had discovered that if she and the kids came home and she said, *I just need twenty minutes, then I can hang with you guys,* and immediately started to empty lunchboxes, put the laundry in, and do the other items on her to-do list, it would end in chaos and she'd spend double the amount of time trying to get her kids back into balance. Instead, she tried giving her kids twenty minutes of undivided attention (letting the lunchboxes and piles of shoes and dishes be), and then starting dinner and picking up the house. Her kids felt better and the whole evening flowed more smoothly.

Nature. Being in nature has been found to lower levels of stress hormones, improve mood, and increase cognitive abilities. One study found that gardening for thirty minutes significantly reduced stress chemicals, even more than thirty minutes of reading. Another found that walking in nature reduced activity in the part of the brain responsible for rumination (continuously thinking about things that upset you). That means nature can often get us "unstuck." Being in green spaces is mentally and physically good for us. Practicing mindfulness (page 88) in nature is a double positive: Notice the branches, admire the flowers, track the clouds as they move across the sky. Go out at night and find the moon, or look at the stars. Shift focus to what your kids notice outside that you probably wouldn't notice on your own: the pebbles lining the flower patch or the caterpillar crawling along the branch.

Leave while you're having fun. Let's say you're at a party and, for the first time in weeks, you're catching up with friends or family, reveling in grown-up conversation, and being out of your humdrum routine. It feels amazing, so you push it just a bit further. Next thing you know, you've been out way longer than you planned, it's past bedtime, and the kids have consumed nothing but frosted cookies and juice boxes. This is when things fall apart. In an overstimulated, undernourished zone, kids' patience and reason are gone and you are faced with crankiness, resistance, and possibly full-on tantrums. It can take days for children to make up for lost sleep, so emotional fragility and stuck moments are common in the days following a big night. If you can, decide ahead of time when it would make sense to leave an event, and do your best to stick to it. There will be times when you're sacrificing an hour of fun, but if everyone feels balanced, you can look forward to your next outing instead of dreading the aftermath.

RESTAURANTS
BABY STEPS, WITH HIGH EXPECTATIONS

We take for granted all the etiquette and social behaviors that go in to being in a restaurant. It's a complex set of rules and expectations! A lot of parents feel nervous or avoid restaurants with babies and little kids, but we want you to do the opposite. Eating in a restaurant takes practice, and if you avoid it, your child won't have good experiences to build on. On the other hand, if they learn early, bit by bit, then being a good restaurant-goer becomes like second nature. When kids are little, you may have to order your food when you first arrive at a restaurant and take your child on a little walk while waiting. At the same time, having high expectations, even of toddlers, will help over time.

State the expectations for restaurants:

> *When we're eating, remember we stay on our bottoms or knees. That means we don't go under the table or stand on the bench.*

> *You guys already know this, but I'm reminding you to use an inside voice. Other people are eating and talking.*

> *When the food comes, we put away our drawing materials and other toys. We eat and talk when the food is here. Anyone see any other toys on the table to put in the bag?*

> *When we sit at the table, all our electronics go away. Mom, want to hand me your phone and I'll put it in my bag?*

If restaurants have been tricky, remind your kids of the expectations before you arrive. Eating is a communal family experience, which means it's a chance for everyone to talk to each other. If little kids never use electronics at the dinner table or in restaurants, they won't see it as an option and will have the chance to develop a natural interest and love of being with their favorite people over a meal (see more on screens in chapter 7). Ask for each person to share one high and one low of the day.

If your little one is disturbing other people, use your ALP steps. You may have to kindly remove her from the restaurant for calm down if she's being too loud or disruptive. It's perfectly fine to have big feelings, but they will have to happen outside the restaurant, on the sidewalk or somewhere else, since restaurants and dinner tables are just for eating, talking, laughing, and being together. Don't worry at all if you end up signaling for the check and a to-go box and hightailing it out of there when no one is having fun. The more your kids practice, the better it gets.

FROM HEATHER

I love eating out, so from the time my kids were babies we've eaten regularly at restaurants, and not just "kid-friendly" ones. When they were really little, we had to work the hardest to engage and entertain them (my husband is exceedingly patient and would tie straws together into shapes that occupied them, or take them out to the sidewalk to look for doggies if the food was taking longer), and knew that restaurant trips might be on the brief side. Now, I always have a pack of markers and notebooks. I had a feeling that having high standards for restaurants—always sitting when the food came, clearing the table of toys or drawing materials, and never using electronics—would pay off in the long run. Eating out together is one of our favorite family activities.

FROM JULIE

When my son was little and I had run out of ideas at a restaurant and desperately wanted to eat my food before it got cold, I would ask the waiter for a glass of ice and a spoon. I put it in front of him and held it firmly with one hand while he got busy trying to spoon up the cubes. I would eat my food with my other hand. For sure a few ended up on the floor but it was a lifesaver!

Child-Led Play

Child-led play is a powerful and simple tool (so simple it's actually hard to do!). If you incorporate the ideas of child-led play, you'll see how it shifts your focus in a positive way, lessens power struggles, and helps your child become more emotionally regulated. Adopting the ideas, even just in a small way every day, will strengthen your relationship with your child.

The key in child-led play is to *follow*. This sounds simple, but for most of us, it's really not. We're used to making decisions, solving problems, relaying information, answering questions, and giving directions. Our minds are full of to-dos, so it's hard to clear away the noise enough to focus, watch, and take a backseat. Sometimes it's also hard not to get bored (how many train cars can you possibly link and vroom?) because the game may seem pointless or simple to you, but try to stay with your child for a short period and see where his ideas take you.

Children are little scientists, and their brains are primed to seek information based on the developmental skills they're working on. This means their natural interests are very important, because they drive a child to conduct just the right experiments. Your role in child-led play is to be curious about what your little one is interested in, striving toward, or struggling with.

For Babies and Young Toddlers

You feed them, bathe them, change their diapers, dress them, move their bodies in and out of car seats, high chairs, and strollers, and decide what they can and cannot touch. When it comes to daily life, it's your choice, your timing, and little kids pretty much have no say in the matter. Yes, this is essential and you wouldn't be a good parent if you didn't do this. But if we don't consciously give little kids some control and time to show us what *they* want to do and explore, their tolerance for all the time you are in charge runs out quickly.

Babies and kids have a strong and natural need to show their favorite people (us) who they are and what they love. They need to see that we notice and share in their delight, which for babies could be as simple as a cardboard box or a cool-shaped stick. By giving them regular opportunities to show us, their need is satisfied.

How-tos for Babies and Young Toddlers

Set aside one or two twenty-minute periods of time during the day to try this practice. Let your baby know when it begins and ends. You can say something like, *Let's see what you're into right now. Show me what you're working on. Can I join you on the ground?* (Yes, say this even before you think your baby can understand!)

- Create a safe space where you won't have to limit set.
- Set out a few simple toys or objects.
- Turn off your devices and put away your phone.
- Take a deep breath and focus on the moment.
- Wait, watch, and follow what your child does, resisting the urge to correct or teach. If he's interested in his hands, look at his hands too. If he's working on rolling, watch him do it. If he brings out trains, notice and follow.
- Join in the play without taking over. Narrate and ask questions to help him follow through on his plans and expand on his ideas.
- Reflect back to him all of his emotions—the happy ones *and* the sad or frustrated ones. Use your facial expression, your body language, and, at times, your words.

- Be aware of not talking constantly. Nonverbal communication and silence lets your child be the one to take the lead.

If your toddler is mobile, child-led play will look different and often will be more active. One little boy we know was obsessed with brooms. Wherever he and his mom went, he looked for a broom. In the grocery store parking garage and the local library, they discovered where the broom was stored and pulled it out and swept. Who knows what this little boy was working on—maybe a physics experiment and probably a fascination with using a tool to complete a task. As a parent, you often won't know exactly what they're learning, but this mom understood that to her son in these moments, being able to use the broom meant the world. So when they weren't in a rush, she'd stop and let him sweep until he was ready to move on.

FROM HEATHER: BUTTERFLY FRUSTRATIONS

One day, my daughter was trying to make little paper butterflies. She was working hard at it, but they wouldn't turn out the way she wanted, so she said, "I'm bad at this. I'll never be able to do these," and started to tear up. I wanted to say, "You're doing great! You're so smart and perfect!" (which is all true), but instead I said, "It's frustrating cutting these small papers. You have an idea in your head and it's hard to make it happen with the paper." She nodded and looked a little relieved. I said, "The papers are small, I can see that. You're really working on it," and slowed down to watch her. "Hm. I notice the paper gets really thick when it's folded up a lot." She folded and refolded and kept working on it until she figured out a way that worked. Reflecting her feelings and sportscasting gave her the relief and comfort she needed to keep trying and a small observation gave her a new idea to try.

For Kids

By *not* teaching, initiating, or overhelping, you allow your child not only to learn more and become more independent, but also to experience the thrill of having an idea and following through with it—all while making natural mistakes. This sense of agency and control over your own life has major benefits, and it's very important that we give our kids an increasing amount of it as they grow. Research shows that people who feel in control (the opposite of feeling helpless) are significantly less anxious or depressed. They feel a fundamental sense of optimism and ability to persevere—because it comes from the inside, not because they've been told what to do all the time. Letting your child have times in which you follow his natural interests without teaching (as well as allowing him to make decisions, take responsibility for school work, and so forth) is part of this process.

How-tos for Kids

Let go of your agenda and redirect your focus to what your preschooler or school-age child is looking at, working on, or interested in. Say, *Hey, can we do some playtime where you show me what you're working on?*

- Turn off your devices.
- Watch and listen to your child. If you feel your thoughts go to drafting a work e-mail in your mind, or wondering

what's in the refrigerator, that's okay. Move your thoughts and attention back to what's in front of you.

- Follow what she's doing. Do the same thing alongside her or add to her project.
- Ask questions about the characters or plot. Take on a role if invited to imaginary play.
- Wonder aloud what she's thinking about.
- Resist the urge to correct and teach.

For older children, digging in with them and learning about their favorite topics goes a long way. Lean into what your child loves (even if it's garbage trucks, subway trains, or tea parties). You may not love it too, but you will know your child better and learn a lot along the way. You might find something fascinating about it and naturally get into it with them. Having children means you get to learn all kinds of information again, or for the first time. Do you remember the names of every planet and the order they go from the sun? Do you know the rules of baseball—if you watch a season you'll probably get into it. Now you can talk and share interests with your kids. Helping them follow through on those interests, however random and seemingly small, builds their brain's ability to focus, learn, and persevere.

FROM JULIE

I have such vivid memories of what it felt like to simply say yes to playing catch with my son. At first it felt so hard to pry myself away from my tasks, but the minute we started throwing the ball back and forth, everything shifted. Our connection to each other was instantly stronger, my sense of humor returned, and I felt peaceful. The little frictions between us dissolved. Who cared about the e-mails, the laundry, or the cooking? What could matter more than this feeling of balance, rhythm, and simple sweet connection to my son? I learned to not resist these invitations, knowing what they would bring.

FROM HEATHER

I grew up in a college town and went to basketball games a lot, but I hadn't watched the game in decades when my son suddenly became a massive LeBron James fan. The desire came from him, but my husband and I followed, and within one season the whole family, including his four-year-old sister, would be cheering and yelling at the TV.

Tools for Adults

When kids are having a tantrum, yelling at a sibling, not listening to you, or whining, it can be really hard to manage your own anger and frustration. If you yell or engage in power struggles, though, it escalates the conflict. If you can stay calm, or at least remove yourself until you are, the problem becomes easier to solve, and your relationship with your child will benefit.

When You Want to Yell

It's hard to stay calm and communicate well when you're flooded with anger and frustration. For some parents, this is absolutely the most challenging part of ALP. Here are some ways to help. Go to our website, nowsaythisbook.com, for a printable version of these tools.

Where do you feel it in your body? Your jaw clenched, your heart beating faster, starting to sweat or get slightly hot, tension in your neck, rolling your eyes, squinting, scrunching up your shoulders—what are the signs that you're getting upset? If you're attuned to yourself, you will be in much better control of what to do next.

Use self-talk. Choose one statement or question to say in your mind. For example,

> *What is she really telling me right now with her behavior?*
>
> *I'm not a bad parent. I'm having normal feelings.*
>
> *She is not manipulating me. She's showing that something is difficult for her right now.*
>
> *It's my job to stay calm and be the bigger person.*
>
> *To her, this moment is huge. This feels like the end of the world to her.*
>
> *I can steer this ship through calm waters and stormy ones.*

Jot down your own helpful self-talk:

_____

_____

_____

_____

_____

Visualize big feelings as waves. It's okay for feelings to unsettle you, but they don't have to capsize your boat. Remember your storm analogy from chapter 1. Take a deep breath and don't say anything immediately unless you have to. The first words out of your mouth may not be the ones you really want to say. Imagine the waves rolling under you, rather than hitting you straight on. Intense emotions often soften within ninety seconds.

Remove yourself from the situation if you need to. Say something like,

> *I need to take space for a few seconds. I'll be right back. I need a calm-down moment.*

You can be transparent with your feelings to a degree, especially with older kids. Say,

> *You know, I'm starting to feel frustrated. I'm asking you to put on your shoes and I see it's not happening. You know that feeling, when you're waiting for someone and they're not moving and you feel stuck?*

> *I need to take a second here. Let's talk about this in a minute. I need to sort this out in my mind.*

You're not perfect, and it's okay for your kids to know that. There's a balance to this, however, because you don't want to abandon your child in the middle of a hard moment or make her worry about you. It's good that your kids see you being comfortable expressing feelings and attuning to yourself (remember, ALP works in all directions), but also that they have a sense of you as being capable. So air the resolution, not just the problem. For example,

> *I was feeling frustrated, but I think I have an idea. When I took a break, I realized we didn't plan this right. Let's start over.*

Put a cap on the conversation or exit. You don't have to continue talking if you've done your three ALP steps.

> *I'm going to explain it again, but then I'm not going to talk about it anymore.*

If you do lose your temper, it's important to "repair." See "Repair and Circle Back" (page 52).

Think about where your reactions come from. A thorough exploration of your childhood is outside the scope of this book, but start by asking yourself these questions:

> What particular behaviors in your child bother you? How do they make you feel? Can you make sense of why?
>
> Is there a quality or behavior of your child's that reminds you of yourself (and makes you overreact)?
>
> Does your child feel very different from yourself or from your expectations? Does this make it hard to let her be who she is?
>
> Does it feel scary to let go of control of your child, even in moments when you know it's okay to?
>
> Did your parents yell or get angry quickly when you were a kid?
>
> What are your preconceived notions of being a par-

ent? What kind of expectations of parenthood do you have?

Are you able to be kind and accepting with yourself when you make a mistake or are you hard on yourself?

Are you sleeping well, eating well, exercising, and connecting with people who will listen and empathize with you? Our kids need us to take care of ourselves so that we can take care of them. See "Filling Your Own Tank" on the next page.

Practice mindfulness on a daily basis. Practice the mindfulness exercises in the next section.

EXAMPLE: MOM ATTUNES TO HERSELF TO GET THROUGH A HARD MOMENT

Tracy was coming home with her kids. She unloaded the car and ended up with ten objects, bags, toys, and pairs of shoes dripping off her as she headed in the door, and meanwhile everyone needed something. "Mama, we're having mac 'n' cheese for dinner tonight, right?" "Mama, I can't find the game on TV yet, where is it?" She could feel her tension rising and she felt overwhelmed. This was a moment when she might have snapped, so she decided to sportscast her feelings and take a time-out. "Guys, you know what, I can feel myself getting frustrated, and as you can see I have tons of things in my hands. I can't answer any questions this second. Please check back with me in a few." She was able to monitor herself and take a little space. The questions stopped before she got too anxious.

Find Someone to Talk to

If you yell, feel angry or heated, and have a hard time staying open and understanding most of the time, you would probably benefit from seeing a therapist to explore your triggers and give you more tools. It can make all the difference in the world to have someone to understand *you*. When parents are listened to, they're better able to listen to their children. It's normal to "mess up" over and over, but if it feels almost impossible to employ ALP, that's a sign you could use more support. In our practice, we coach and support parents, because shifting to ALP can be challenging at first.

Filling Your Own Tank

When you take care of yourself, your kids benefit. You have more patience, you're less distracted, and you have more humor and better creative problem-solving skills.

This is no easy task. So often, parents feel they simply don't have the time to even think about their own needs, much less do anything about them. We get it—it feels like a big juggling act. Small changes to your self-care and the balance in your life will reap long-term benefits. Look at this list and find one to start with. Make a small improvement on it tomorrow. The day after tomorrow, continue on with that improvement and add one more to it.

Sleep thirty minutes more per night. Sleep changes everything. Try a few simple healthy sleep habits. Go to bed at the same time every night (as much as humanly possible). If it's hard to wake up when the alarm goes off, go to bed ten minutes earlier every night until you're waking up refreshed. Do not look at your computer or phone for sixty minutes before getting into bed, even to just "check," and keep your phone out of your bedroom. Use a regular alarm without a digital light, because it's better to have total darkness and not check the time in the night. If you're not sleeping well, avoid regularly consuming alcohol before bed. Wear a sleep mask if you're waking up too early in the morning. If you're not sleeping because your child is not sleeping, implement the effective strategies in *The Happy Sleeper*.

Feed yourself as you'd want your kids to eat. Pack yourself a healthy lunch and snacks along with those for your kids. Keep it simple. Try not to skip meals or turn to sweet, less healthy alternatives out of desperation. Divvy up dinner prep with your partner and kids. Eat sitting down without distraction.

Ask your friends and family for help. Who are the people who really listen to you? We work with parents all the time to lend support and guidance. We're continually impressed by the enormity of their tasks and roles and how tirelessly they strive to be the best parents they can be. Sharing after-school care, playdates, driving, and more with other parents not only lightens your load, it's more fun and it's how you build your "village." We are communal creatures. Since most of us live in separate homes these days, we have to consciously create ways to connect with other families. Reaching out for help is an important life skill and one that many of us need to intentionally make an effort to acquire. It sounds funny to have to make an effort to ask for help, but it's true, many of us need to adjust our belief system for this one.

Clear and Calm Your Mind—Mindfulness

We have a powerful tool to use in our win-win parenting approach: mindfulness. Mindfulness is a practice both old and new. People have practiced mindfulness for thousands of years, and more recently, its positive effects on health and well-being have been demonstrated through psychological and neuroscience research. There are many ways to define mindfulness. Here is one of our favorite definitions, from researcher and author Jon Kabat-Zinn. Mindfulness is:

- paying attention
- on purpose
- in the present moment
- without judgment

The practice of mindfulness is central to this book. When you are mindful, you focus on what is in front of you and let go of distractions, to-do lists, negative thoughts, worries, and more. Mindfulness has been shown to reduce stress levels, improve cognition and attention, help children with ADHD, and improve school performance.

Here, we will give you some ideas for exercises to help you and your children flex and strengthen the mental muscles of mindfulness. This is a practice, a way of being that takes time to develop. Think of it as strengthening a muscle that you especially need in difficult moments. If you've done your exercises, your muscle is strong and poised to help when you need it the most. People who practice mindfulness regularly have a longer fuse, a better ability to see the other's perspective, and tend to choose thoughtfully how to respond to a difficult, emotional moment.

Mindfulness helps you attune. You connect with your child's internal mental world and are open to what is really happening with her in the moment. If you can hear and understand your child in her most vulnerable, challenging states, this unconditional love builds a sense of trust and safety that she will carry with her forever. Mindfulness also helps you set limits. It allows you to consciously choose your responses, rather than react from a knee-jerk, automatic stance.

Mindfulness shifts you from

Knee-jerk		Attuned
Automatic		Receptive
	to	
Reactive		Intentional
Thoughtless		Thoughtful

When we are mindful as parents, we also cultivate and nourish our attachment relationships with our babies and kids as they grow. The more present we are, the more our children trust us and the more securely attached they become—this helps them grow naturally more independent over time.

The great news is that mindfulness goes in all directions. Use it with your child, but also with your partner, family, friends, strangers, and yourself. We say "yourself," because you can use mindfulness to be aware of, kind, and patient with yourself. This helps you extend this way of being to the people around you.

Mindfulness Exercises

The key is to choose something that fits into daily life, whether it's joining a class, practicing yoga, listening to guided meditations, or choosing a simple daily meditation. Set yourself up for success, rather than having one more thing that you feel bad about not getting to each day. Here are a few very simple, doable, and even fun ideas.

Observe Your Child

This one is simple and rewarding. Stop doing what you're doing and look, listen, and take in your baby or child. Watch him for five or ten minutes and resist the urge to do or change (unless he's upset). Take a deep breath and try to imagine what he is doing, what he wants and doesn't want, and what he is feeling. Let it all be okay. We do this in our Mommy and Me classes and it always shifts the dynamic in the room to one of calm, awe, and togetherness.

Walking and Listening Meditation

You can do this exercise while walking anywhere, or even pushing a stroller along the street, down the hall, up the hill. Turn your focus to sounds. Notice every variety of sound you hear while you're walking. An airplane flying overhead, your feet on the sidewalk, a dog barking, a whizzing car, a buzz in the background, a conversation next to you. If you start thinking about something else, shift your focus back to the sounds. Do this for five minutes one day, and build up your time until you reach twenty minutes at a time. When you feel overwhelmed and distracted, start this meditation, and, over time, it will become easier because the mental pathways are stronger.

Water and Feeling Meditation

You can do this while washing the dishes, taking a shower, or watering the plants. Let your mind tune in to the feel of the water on your skin, the sensations of suds, the temperature. Let go of thoughts about the past or what will happen later today and just focus on the feeling of water. Imagine that the water sweeps away the negative thoughts and worries in your mind. You can add the previous listening meditation so you're listening to the water sounds.

Morning Meditation

Let's face it, lying in bed may be one of the few times you have to yourself. No one has to know you're awake. Just take five minutes to lie or sit in your bed with your eyes closed and notice your breath going in and out. Slow it down a little. You can even add a little mantra. "Let" on the inhale and "go" on the exhale is one example. Make up your own. Don't overthink it. Just do five minutes each day, very simple, and see how it goes.

Take Off Your Filters

Babies and kids do this naturally. They take in many more details in their environment. We tend to filter out a lot and miss nuance, beauty, and details that would inform us. Try looking around you, in the coffee shop or store, as you walk down the street, when you come into your home at the end of the day. What do you see, hear, smell, notice? Try changing the route you take home or to school every day to one that you haven't seen before, or that is more pleasant. While you walk, notice everything in front of you.

Be Mindful Together

Practice simple meditations and relaxation tools with your kids when everything is calm. Then you can pull them out when things go awry and your kids' brains will be primed to move to a calmer, more open place, regulate emotions, and be able to accept the limit while exploring acceptable alternatives. You could play a meditation recording during your kids' bedtime routine and lie in the dark together for five minutes listening. You can include them in the examples here and create some just for them. Some kids like lying down with a stuffed animal on their belly, watching it go up and down as they breathe slowly. Others love body-scan techniques, where they tense one part of their body at a time on the inhale and then let it go on the exhale.

Make it a new way of being around something you're already doing, so you don't really have to add one more thing to your day. When things get tough, try to bring yourself back to how you feel during your simple meditations. Does it get easier over time to slow down, become curious, take in your child, and decide thoughtfully how to respond? Be patient with yourself—this takes time.

Attune in Easier Moments

Attuning is a way of being, not just for difficult moments. The more your kids feel that you're present and interested when they're not melting down or breaking a rule, the less likely you are to have those bumpy moments in the first place, because you're starting from a more connected way of being together. When kids act out, they're often seeking our attention and approval. If they can't get it for happily playing on their own, they'll find another way that works.

Turn off devices during mealtime, walks to and from school, and bedtime routines; spend time sitting on the floor and playing with your kids; look them in the eyes and let them talk without rushing them; listen to their crazy stories from preschool. Now we're "filling the tank," and they'll weather the emotional bumps much better. This is true whether you're a working parent who has one hour, or a stay-at-home parent. Sometimes they just need to know you see them, even without words, or with a simple *I saw that!* A glance at their drawing or Lego creation, a witness to their leaping-off-the-step feat. Don't be afraid that you'll break the spell and lose your alone time. That may happen at first, but as your children come to trust that you are present and interested, they will feel content to play independently.

Difficult Feelings and Tantrums

No matter how nonsensical and frustrating our child's feelings may seem to us, they are real and important to our child. It's vital that we treat them as such in our response.

—Daniel J. Siegel and Tina Payne Bryson

It's the moment you dread, when your child becomes unreasonable, irrational, or flooded with emotions. The tiniest things will push kids over the edge. Your toddler screams at the injustice of not being able to take home the fluorescent stuffed animal from the grocery store. Your preschooler sobs because you unwrapped the fruit roll-up when *she wanted to do it.* (How dare you!) Your third-grader throws an epic tantrum because you turned off the iPad.

Meltdowns, outbursts, tantrums, and other expressions of "negative" emotions are incredibly normal, and in the next section we'll explain why they happen. But you don't really need us to tell you tantrums are normal. You've heard that before, and it's pretty clear from looking around you that it's true. In our practice, we realized over the years that normalizing negative feelings and emotional floods isn't enough. It gives parents reassurance, but they continue to try and cut off feelings quickly, correct right away, or coax their kids into being happy again.

Knowing that tantrums are normal can bring you comfort, but seeing them as an *opportunity* can be a revelation. This will change the way you relate to your child, and also how you relate to your own feelings. Frustration, anger, sadness, and tantrums are not just unfortunate facts of life for little kids, they are small doors that continuously open, every day. When a door opens, we have a chance to say, with our words, tone, and body language, "Your feelings are accepted by me. I see you, and I'm interested." How we respond in those moments affects how our children feel about themselves and our relationship (Does my most important person get me? Are my big feelings safe here?) and also how they make sense of, manage, and regulate those feelings. Every day, babies and toddlers are practicing emotional skills with our help, and those daily interactions are their training ground.

We're moms, so we understand why you would dread emotional drama. And we aren't saying it's easy to flip your thinking about negative feelings—or even that you'll accomplish it every time. Some days you'll only find one door, while the other moments feel like a struggle. That's great. Open one door every day—that's what it means to practice.

Often when kids lose control of their feelings, cry, or throw themselves to the ground kicking and screaming, it feels like an assault to us, a failure on our part, or even a manipulation. But the very moment when your child is being as unappealing and unhinged as she can possibly be is the moment when she's signaling that she needs you the most.

In this chapter, we'll help you practice responding to difficult feelings like sadness, anger, anxiety, and frustration, and also tantrums (or what we would call "emotional floods"), in an attuned way, while also being strong in your role as the parent, teaching and holding limits. This gives kids a sense that they matter (and not just when they're happy and sweet), and that you are there to coach and assist. Over time, the pathways in their brain that manage and make sense of feelings will strengthen, and you'll see your child slowly but surely become more rational and make better choices. The goal is not to make feelings go away, it's to help kids weather life's inevitable waves and emotional storms. With our help, they develop resilience and can handle hard moments and get back on track. This becomes a crucial skill for life.

Why Tantrums Happen: Little People, Big Feelings

Big feelings are a fact of life. Emotions come online early, even in the littlest of babies. Infants express sadness, frustration, anger, joy, fear, and many other emotions, and as children grow, their emotions become more complex and nuanced. As they mature into toddlerhood, feelings like guilt and embarrassment mean kids are becoming self-aware and socially conscious.

This is all good news. Human evolution gave us emotions because they provide us with valuable information. They help us react to the environment and know if something is threatening or desirable. They influence our perception, help us make decisions, and connect us to one another. We need emotions.

The challenge for a parent—who may be simply trying to exit a store with a two-year-old drowning in tears because she can't push the shopping cart—is that the rich, booming emotional life of a young child outpaces rational thought and self-control. Think about what it's like to be overwhelmed by your feelings. Let's say you've unexpectedly lost your job, and you're so shocked and devastated you can hardly focus or think about anything else. Later in the day, you might start thinking with your rational brain about updating your resume, and realizing it's not the end of the world—but in the moment, your feelings are all-consuming. Now imagine going through every day this way, without good emotional brakes, filters, or perspective. Little kids are far more vulnerable to emotional floods and bumpy waters because they're still building the machinery that allows them to steer and control the boat. When a flood, or a tantrum, occurs, the nervous system is overwhelmed and dysregulated, thoughts are not clear, hearts are pounding, and stress hormones rise.

SLEEPY KIDS, FRAGILE EMOTIONS

Sleep is critical to your child's emotional health. The brain's prefrontal cortex is compromised when children don't sleep enough, which makes it harder for them to regulate and manage their emotions. Sleeping just thirty minutes more per night has been shown to decrease children's moodiness and impulsivity. Kids need an average of eleven to twelve hours of sleep. You will find comprehensive strategies to solve any sleep issue for babies to school-age children at TheHappySleeper.com.

Interpreting and regulating emotions is a developmental skill set that takes years (even decades) to acquire. This has a lot to do with time; it's a long, gradual process for these brain regions to intricately connect. It's also influenced by temperament: research shows that some babies are more prone to negative emotions than others. But you, as the parent, also have an influential role. Responding sensitively to babies and toddlers helps them make sense of their experience, and those kids develop better emotional regulation skills.

∼ TALKING TO YOUR BABY ∼

Most of us know that we're supposed to talk to our babies when they're happy and babbling, but talking to them when they're upset is just as important. Applying the ALP steps to difficult moments with your baby shows her that you're interested in her feelings and helps her develop an emotional vocabulary, even from the youngest age. Babies who have an emotional vocabulary can use it later on to express themselves.

INSTEAD OF "YOU'RE OKAY" OR "IT'S OKAY"

If your baby is upset, she's *not* okay and saying this very common phrase misses an opportunity to attune. It's dismissive of her feelings. Instead, say something like,

> *That scared you.*

> *You weren't ready to be put down.*

> *That looked like it hurt. Let me see that arm.*

In some situations, letting your baby have her feelings is all that's called for. If she's crying (and you've ruled out hunger, pain, and so forth), she could just be overwhelmed and having a hard time—it may not be a moment for you to fix anything. At times, babies need to release stress, just like everyone else. If so, try holding her and saying something like,

> *Let it out.*

> *I hear you.*

Oh, this sounds hard.

I'm here with you.

WHERE DID MY SWEET, EASY BABY GO?

At around seven to nine months of age, parents see a real shift in their baby's opinions. This sudden burst of big feelings can come as an unwelcome surprise to parents, as daily moments that never used to be a problem become a source of unhappiness and frustration. In our parenting groups, it's not uncommon to hear parents say something to the effect of "Where did my sweet baby go?" Big feelings arise around diaper changes (which used to be such nice moments of connection), getting dressed, getting in the car seat, really wanting to hold something they can't, or really not wanting to do something they have to.

The silver lining is that this shift means that cognitively, your baby is right on track. She's becoming more aware, more discerning, and better able to communicate how she feels. Outbursts of emotion, both "positive" and "negative," tell you that your baby's internal life is becoming richer.

Babies have good reason to get frustrated: they see so many things they're not yet able to do or to touch, while lacking the ability to understand why. Imagine you knew you wanted a cup of coffee but couldn't tell anyone clearly and were not allowed to touch the coffeemaker. Your simple desire would quickly turn to frustration. In the second half of the first year, babies also begin to understand language and the gist of communication. They know what they want to say but they can't say it, so they show it by screaming, crying, flailing, and kicking.

Without a well-tuned emotional brake on these big feelings, baby's emotions can easily spiral out of control. In an instant, they reach a point where they cannot get back into balance on their own. They don't mean to do this; it's outside of their ability. This is a good thing to remind yourself of, as these moments can feel like manipulation or excessively irrational behavior.

Babies are able to make sense of what we say to them, much earlier than we think. When we work with parents to help babies sleep, sometimes we ask them to talk to their babies about it. Moms and dads look at us like we're crazy for suggesting telling an eight-month-old that she will have a new bedtime plan, showing her the crib, and explaining how the routine will go, but over time parents see how helpful it is.

EXAMPLE: TALKING BABY THROUGH TUMMY TIME

Mabel hated tummy time, her parents were convinced. We were working with Mabel's parents to help set up good sleep habits for her and, at five months, it was clear that having more motor control and learning to roll would help her sleep. We asked them to show us Mabel's play space. Mom put her on her tummy. Sure enough, Mabel immediately started to cry and scream and Mom plucked her up to a more familiar position. To help Mabel get more comfortable with tummy time, we showed Mom and Dad how to lay Mabel on her back, look her in the eyes, say "I'm going to roll you," and then get down on the ground and talk to Mabel face-to-face. When Mabel complained, her mom would say, "It's frustrating because you're not used to being here," and when she really protested, her mom would guide her in rolling to her back again—molding her instead of plucking her up so that Mabel would feel in control. After a week, Mom wrote us to say that Mabel loved playing on her tummy.

Practicing ALP early is great groundwork. By doing this without placating ("You're okay!") or responding harshly, you nurture your baby's natural tendency to recover, to be empathic to others and themselves, and to feel good about who they are, in all their emotional colors.

In the scripts section at the end of this chapter, you'll see examples for young babies, and also be sure to read about using child-led play on page 76 as the antidote to a day full of limit setting and frustration.

Emotional floods also happen because little ones know what they want far before they can articulate it, and other people are doing all kinds of cool things they can't do yet. Not only that, they're controlled by us and told what to do *constantly*: when to leave, where to go, what's okay to do and what not to do, what's okay to touch and what not to touch.

MY CHILD IS EASY AND WELL BEHAVED AT SCHOOL BUT AN EMOTIONAL MESS AT HOME

Good news—you're doing your job! When your child is out in the world, she's working hard to manage her feelings. When she's with you, she's reached a safe touch-point and can let it all go. School is a place to hold it together—home is a place to work things out. If reports from school and sports teams are that she's doing great, but at home she's more sensitive, emotional, or defiant, that's normal—she's expressing herself with the people she trusts most. We'd be more concerned about a kid who is reined in at home but acting out at school.

From our point of view as grown-ups, our kids' tears, insistence, and strong reactions can seem unwarranted. Your preschooler *absolutely must* have the plastic Spider-Man figure in the bathtub, but you you can only find the Batman one. Disaster! In his little world, this plan was all-important—his powers of imagination had created a narrative for Spider-Man, so the other superheroes are irrelevant. It doesn't mean you have to spend twenty minutes scouring the toy bins for Spidey, it just means his feelings are not so out of proportion when we see the world through his eyes.

Parents' Knee-Jerk Reactions

What's your automatic reaction when your toddler has a tantrum and flings her broccoli on the ground, or your kindergartner declares you the meanest mommy in the world, says he hates you, and storms into his room? Most of the "knee-jerk reactions" below are understandable, because we're parents, we care, and we're deeply intertwined with our kids' feelings. We want them to be happy, so it's hard to let it be okay when they're not. We all have different ways of dealing with that uncomfortable sense that our children—the little people we love so much—are having a hard moment.

Anger

Some parents get angry when their kids are emotional, and they yell things like *You're going to time-out if you say that again. I've had enough! Listen or there will be a consequence!* These parents may have very little patience or tolerance for feelings, and are quick to get mad and try to stop their children by yelling or snapping. Often, they were spoken to this way when they were children and feel it's their job to be strict. They don't have a lot of experience being comfortable with big feelings.

"I HATE YOU!"

What do you say when your child says this to you? Shift from looking at the tip of the iceberg, which would focus you on your own hurt feelings or the disrespectfulness of the statement. Instead, address what this developing person is trying to tell you.

REACTIVE (NOT ATTUNED) RESPONSES:

Hey, not okay! Do not talk to me that way!

Go to your room!

That hurts my feelings! I don't want you to say that.

ATTUNED RESPONSES:

Wow, you're really mad at me.

I hear you, you're upset about this.

It's understandable, because it's hard to see our kids upset, especially when they're misbehaving at the same time. Under our own anger is often fear—fear that we're not getting it right or that we're not a good parent.

When you get angry, your child's brain responds with "fight or flight."

When you react with anger, you trigger the basic fear centers in your child's brain. You may not see it this way, but your tone, body position, yelling, or scolding is perceived by your child as a threat, and it causes a stress response in his body. Your anger tells him that he's not safe, and he should fight back, run away, or freeze up and repress his feelings. Being yelled at can start a cascade of physiological events in your child's body: stress hormones rise, muscles tense, and his heart beats faster. Even if you don't raise your voice, your body language (stiff, harsh movements, standing over your child with hands on hips, and so forth) can still convey anger. Over time, if kids are scorned or shamed for their feelings, they begin to see themselves as innately bad, and have lower self-esteem. It becomes a cycle: fear on the part of the parent that he or she is raising a bad kid; fear and shame on the part of the child from the parent's reaction.

A mom gave us a good example of working to change her angry reactions to her toddler's behavior: One evening, he was flailing and crying because, after telling him not to splash water outside the tub, he still soaked the bathroom floor. She had to lift him out kicking and screaming. She was angry at him for being disobedient and then crying about it, irritated by the loud noise, frustrated she'd told him this a hundred times, and worried that she was failing. In the past, when she scolded him, it would escalate her son's distress and they would both end up more upset. She had been practicing the tools outlined on pages 81–85. She took a deep breath and stayed quiet (knowing that if she opened her mouth too quickly she'd regret it), kindly but decisively lifted her son out of the tub, wrapped him in a towel, and took him to a room that was less noisy. When he calmed down enough to hear her, she dug deep to find a firm but soothing voice to say:

You really were not ready to get out, I know. We cannot soak the bathroom floor. I had to move you out of the bathtub. (This is also an example of a follow-through choice.) *Take a deep breath with me.*

Of course, her son was still angry, but it didn't escalate, and she felt good about her calm and firm plan.

Dismiss or Sweep It under the Rug

Other parents try to nip emotional explosions in the bud. These parents might say "Stop it." "It's not okay to say that." "What are you so upset about, it's not a big deal!" in a "no, no, no" voice. We've even heard parents say things like "I don't like hearing you cry—can you go somewhere else and do that?"

Excessively Worry or Make It about Yourself

A client one of us worked with in therapy shared a lot about his relationship with his well-meaning but anxious mom when he was little. His mom didn't get mad at him for being upset; instead, she worried, hovered, and got very upset herself. She asked excessive questions when she suspected something was wrong. He described as a child losing an especially challenging soccer game, after which his mom ran out onto the field devastated and crying. Moments like that made him feel as though *he* now had to take care of *her*. She hijacked his feelings.

Placate or Cave

All of us have this reaction sometimes. We get so worried that our kids are upset or we want so badly for them to feel good that we don't give them the sense it's okay to have ups and downs. This can take the form of placating, giving in, or not holding an expectation or social rule for our kids.

Oh, don't worry, I'll do it for you.

Oh, never mind, okay. We can keep swinging, we don't have to go home.

It's okay, he can run around the restaurant yelling—he doesn't know better.

I know she hit your child, but she's only two—it's normal.

All of these reactions—getting mad, sweeping feelings under the rug, taking them on for ourselves, or placating—are in some way resisting the simple practice of letting feelings be feelings. Remember from page 26 that this means, over time, the child may stop expressing anger and sadness and internalize it, or act it out in other ways.

Instead, when your child expresses a "negative" feeling or has a meltdown, imagine the feelings as waves that come and go. The more okay you are with them, the better. This does not mean you accept *all behaviors*, it just means you accept your child in all her crazy expressions. The sea of life has waves and this is perfectly normal. Rather than praying for a tantrum-free day, wake up every morning wondering what the day will bring and what you'll learn and figure out. You are not in control of everything your child does, nor do we want our kids to feel pressured to always be happy. We want to equip them with a sense that feelings come and go and we can ride those emotional waves and get back on track.

ALP for Difficult Feelings

In this section we'll use ALP with difficult feelings and emotional floods. We will build on the concepts from chapter 1, with a specific focus on feelings.

ALP FOR DIFFICULT FEELINGS

Attune: Let your child know you understand. Depending on what the moment calls for, pause, get on her level, say what you see or hear, paraphrase, or say, "tell me more." Give her space or move to a safe, quiet environment if needed.

It's hard to leave the park; you're sad we have to go.

Limit set: State the limit and brief reason, or state the reality.

We do have to leave because it's getting dark.

Problem solve: Offer a way or ways to solve the dilemma, help your child recover, or make an acceptable choice. Be creative and use humor. Use a follow-through choice if necessary.

Do you want to skip out holding hands, or do you want a piggyback?

I'm going to move your body somewhere safe and quiet.

Attune

Lead with empathy. A short, attuned moment tells your child that his desires and big feelings are acceptable (even though the behavior may not be). You're telling him, *You can come to me with this and I won't get mad, dismiss, judge, or try to fix it. I'll listen.* If your two-year-old can trust you with his feelings now, he's more likely to do the same when he is older.

Don't confuse attuning with overtalking, indulging, letting unacceptable behaviors go, or changing your limit. You can hold a limit and problem solve, all the while validating your child's experience.

Some kids are very watchful and sensitive, and they feel understood with the most subtle glance and acknowledgment. Other kids are harder to reach, so they need a bigger response from you, in which you really emphasize your words and mirror their tone and intensity. Tailor the attune step to your kid's age and temperament. Think, *What does it really take for my kid to feel that I "get" him?*

You may use one of the attune tools each time or combine them. Find the ones that fit the moment. There will be times when attuning is all you need. In other cases, you'll add the limit-setting and problem-solving steps too.

Attune Tool #1:
Pause

Your preschooler erupts into tears. Maybe you know why, or maybe you don't. Many of us say something right away, like *Ah, all right, what is it now?* or *What? What happened? What's the big deal?* or *Oh, you're okay!* Instead, pause and let the crying or yelling be okay for a second. Imagine the waves moving your boat and let that be fine. If no one is in danger, and if the social setting doesn't call for an immediate response (like screaming in a restaurant), you don't have to respond right away. If it's not an urgent moment, you can kneel down and say something like

Oh, hm . . .

Whoa, you have a big feeling about that.

I see.

Attune Tool #2:
I'm Going to Kindly Move You

When it comes to tantrums, how you respond depends on where you are. Are you in a busy restaurant, in a quiet boutique, at the park, or at home? If you're in a public place where the noise is disturbing to others or the environment is overstimulating, let your child know you're going to move her to a quiet place to take a breather. You can respectfully do this, while still sending the message that her feelings are not a problem. If it looks like she might hurt herself or someone else, move the object away or gently hold her body. People might expect you to reprimand your child in public for having an outburst, but don't succumb to this. It's a caring and kind practice to follow as a parent, to move your child to a private spot (the car, another room, the sidewalk, etc.) when she's having a hard time. This avoids shame and embarrassment while giving you a chance to talk somewhere private.

On the other hand, if she's safe and you're not out in public, you may just want to let her stay where she is, while the emotions run their course. Say something like

I see how upset you are. I'm here when you're ready to talk or make a choice.

Read "Why not to ignore a tantrum" on page 114.

Attune Tool #3:
Use Your Body Language

Regardless of the words you say, standing over your child with a frown on your face can make her feel vulnerable, angry, defensive, and more likely to resist.

Getting on eye level or below is enough to signify that you're interested and accepting, even without words. Squatting down changes the power dynamic because you are with your child, not judging or threatening. An open and curious facial expression also makes a big difference. Even though you may still need to set a limit or give information your child doesn't want to hear, your body language will make it easier for her to take it all in.

～ WHY NOT TO IGNORE A TANTRUM ～ OR PUNISH WITH A TIME-OUT

We'd like to address some of the traditional ways of responding to tantrums. You may have been told to ignore a tantrum to make it go away. The idea is that paying attention to kids who are upset rewards them for this behavior. By now you can see why we think this doesn't make sense at all. When kids are having a hard time (even when it seems totally irrational), they're telling us they need us. Ignoring them, punishing them, or giving a time-out is the opposite of this. It makes them feel isolated, cut off, and shamed.

Since tantrums are big expressions of emotion and thought, and signal dysregulation of the nervous system, you need to help your child regulate. How you do this depends on the moment and his personality. If he accepts being held, then hold your child, or put your hand on his back and let him know you hear how upset he is. Some kids are soothed by physical touch—hugging will help them regroup and calm down. If your child is one of these, you might even put your arms out and ask, *I see. Can I give you a hug?* To which he might move toward you and collapse in your arms. If that's the case, offer the squeeze.

Other times, kids need space to ride an emotional wave. Some kids don't like to be touched when they're upset (just like adults, everyone has their preference), and especially if your child is upset at you, then he may not want you to hug him. If you can tell that he's unreachable and nothing you say or do seems to help, then as long as he's safe and not destroying anything, give him space. Say something like

> *I understand. You really wanted the blocks and I put them away because they're not for throwing. I get it. I'm here. (You're not bringing the blocks back out, but you're fine with his feelings about it.)*

You could stay in the same room, or go somewhere close by and check in with him periodically to let him know you're still there in spirit. This is not a punishment. If you do this in a mad or frustrated way, or give the feeling that you're rushing him or hoping it all ends soon, it defeats the purpose of allowing feelings to happen and be released. Your child might even cry louder and longer because of your impatient reaction, or he may bottle up the feelings and not express them so you won't be mad. These ideas should be thought of as a calm down (page 49).

If he's able to listen and isn't crying too hard, you could keep talking. Once you've attuned, state the limit or reality and then move on to the problem-solving step. For example,

> Attune: *I can hear that. You're upset about not having another fruit roll-up. You really like them.* Limit set: *But it's not snack time now, because dinner is soon.*

Problem solve: *Okay, I'm going to give you some space, but I have some ideas when you're ready to talk about it.*

Attune: *I get it, I can see how sad you are about not being able to go play at Sophie's house. I know you were really looking forward to it.* Limit set: *Unfortunately we cannot go today. There's too much to do with home-work and practice.* Problem solve: *I'm here and when you're ready, we can make a plan for you to play at Sophie's sometime this weekend.*

WAIT, HUGGING A CHILD WHO'S MISBEHAVING?

Hugging or rubbing the back of a child who's having a tantrum or has misbehaved may seem out of line—isn't that rewarding bad behavior? We're not thinking in those terms. When your child is struggling—and that includes moments when she's hit her sister or broken a toy—she's telling you she's working on a developmental skill or she needs some-thing. She needs connection, teaching, or calm time. Punish-ing doesn't accomplish any of that. As long as you're holding the limit, you're not being "too soft" and your child will learn that you're on her side.

BUT WHAT ABOUT "MANIPULATIVE" TANTRUMS?

Yes, there are definitely times when kids yell and cry in a purposeful, "I'm in control of myself here" way, when they're trying to get you to change your mind or go back on a limit. (It's easy to tell the difference because if you cave on the limit, they recover immediately.) In these times, focus more on repeating the unwavering limit, rather than rubbing her back, holding, and helping your child regulate her emotions (since by definition her emotions aren't really dysregulated to begin with). We'd still challenge you to use the iceberg analogy with a "manipulative" tantrum. Is she engaged in a power struggle with you or a sibling? Is she overwhelmed, tired, or overscheduled? Was she talked down to or excluded at school today? You may not know the reason every time, but even shifting your thinking this way will help you reframe her behavior and relieve the pressure that you have to correct or punish her.

The key with this and with all tantrums is to be resolute in holding the limit. That way, you don't ever have to get mad or reactive; you simply stay strong and accept the big feelings. A kid's job is to test limits. Your kids will learn that when you set a limit, you hold it. Over time, you'll see how valuable this is.

HEAD BANGING

In our experience, head banging is more common than you might think. The evidence shows that kids will not injure themselves seriously and will learn fairly quickly that it doesn't feel good to bang their heads on the ground or other hard surface. If we rush to try to stop them the phase will likely last longer, because they are not getting the input they need to learn to stop doing it. This is really hard behavior to ignore, we know. You can gently move your child if she's on a really hard surface or in a very public place. Just try not to let her know how upsetting the head banging is to you. Give her the sense that you are nearby and ready to help, when she is able to hear you.

Attune Tool #4:
Say What You See: The Sportscaster

Without judging or correcting, simply say what is happening. Remember from chapter 1 that the sportscaster technique helps kids connect cause and effect and think creatively, without feeling blamed and defensive.

Your fists are clenched and your shoulders are up.

I can see, you look frustrated.

Your body is heating up, I can tell.

She got too close to you and her voice was loud. It made you feel crowded.

You were playing with the doll and really didn't want it to get taken away.

In some cases, when you use the sportscaster, your child will come to her own conclusions without your direction. In other cases, especially when kids are little, you'll need your limit-setting and problem-solving steps too.

Attune Tool #5:
Paraphrase: The Good Waiter

It's remarkable how much more you'll learn if you simply say back what your child is telling you, rather than trying to fix or convince her out of her feelings. Therapists are trained to use this technique because it validates and helps people open up. It takes practice, because as parents we want to rush in with our ideas right away. A good waiter listens to you and says it back to make sure she got it right. Whether your child is anxious, feeling slow to warm up or shy, has a complaint about the contents of his lunch box, is mad at a friend, or mad at you—try to get the essence of what he's telling you and say it back in your own words. Wait. See what else comes out.

I don't want to go to school!	(Instead of) *Why? You love school!*
	(Say) *Don't feel like it this morning, huh?*
I'll never be able to make a basket. I can't do it.	(Instead of) *Don't say that—you can do it!*
	(Say) *You've been trying so hard, huh? You're frustrated because it feels like it'll never happen.*
Waaaaa, I want a cookie right now!	(Instead of) *No. No cookies now.*
	(Say) *They look yummy to you.*
I wanna go on the swings, waaaaa!	(Instead of) *You have to be patient!*
	(Say) *It's hard to wait. You're watching from the side and wishing you were on those swings right now.*
Aiden called me a smarty-pants at school today.	(Instead of) *What did you say? Did you tell the teacher? Don't play with him anymore.*
	(Say) *Smarty pants? I bet you didn't like that.*
Waaaaa, you turned off the TV!	(Instead of) *Okay, I'll turn it back on.*
	(Say) *I know, it's hard to stop watching when you're into the show.*

Use "feeling" words when they fit the moment. If you label feelings, your child will grow up with more emotional skill and a rich vocabulary of words to describe emotions. Have you met adults who seem disconnected from their feelings? Talking this way from an early age helps kids become familiar with and accepting of their internal world.

Try not to say a perfunctory *That made you sad,* or just parrot back your child's words. Paraphrasing statements shouldn't come off as condescending, nor should you say the same thing every time. Keep it real and unique to the situation.

FROM JULIE: "MOMMY, I FEEL LIKE HITTING YOU RIGHT NOW!" AND OTHER ACCOMPLISHMENTS

I had a lovely mom in Mommy and Me class who continued to work with me on ALP after the group graduated. When we started working together, she was often in a power struggle with her toddler and found herself reprimanding and nagging him in a critical, aggravated tone. She was impatient and angry and she could tell it was affecting him, because he would yell and hit her. She worked especially hard on changing her tone of voice and empathizing with him while holding limits. She could hear that reprimanding tone the minute it came out of her mouth, even when she was simply saying his name! One day, when her son was just over two years old, he was in an especially fraught power struggle with her. Finally, he said, "Mommy, I feel like hitting you right now." But, he *didn't* hit her. It was an incredible moment and she knew it—it meant he was expressing himself and he was resisting an impulse.

She felt proud of him, and of all her hard work. This little boy was very young to have that level of self-awareness, but that's what we're going for. We want our kids to verbalize their feelings, to tell us how they feel, instead of acting them out. We want them to feel safe expressing all of their feelings to us. We are the parents; we can handle it.

Attune Tool #6:
Tell Me More

Parents often tell us they're worried they'll make it worse if they lean in to emotions, so we hear them try to argue kids out of their feelings. Rather than disagreeing, be curious. Say a phrase or ask a question that makes your child feel receptive and open to talking. This is how you'll find out more and keep the conversation going,

Tell me more about that.

Help me understand, give me more information.

So it feels like . . .

I'm scared of my room.	(Instead of) *There's nothing to be scared of.*
	(Say) *Huh. Really, I didn't know that. What's scaring you about it?*

Attune Tool #7:
Use Your Iceberg Analogy

Using the tools above can often get you to what's beneath the surface. The tip of the iceberg might be crying, kicking, yelling, or whining, but what is going on under the surface, and what is your child telling you? Is he:

- Tired
- Hungry
- Off his schedule
- Overstimulated (in a place that is too loud or has too many lights, other kids, or activity)
- Bored or needing connection
- Overwhelmed, overscheduled, or stressed by school and activities
- Trying to interact or get in the game but not sure how to do it
- Needing time to recover after something challenging happened recently

If so, respond to what's under the surface rather than the behaviors poking out of the water.

You're a meanie!	(Instead of) *That is disrespectful and not allowed!*
	(Say) *Wow, you're super angry at me.*

EXAMPLE: PLAYDATE CONFLICT

Charlie is at a playdate and is crying, whining, provoking, and not getting along with his buddy.

Tip-of-the-iceberg response: *Why aren't you being nice to Emma? Stop crying. Do you need a time-out? We're going to leave if you don't play nicely.*

Beneath-the-surface response: (Parent knows Charlie wel enough to see he's trying to engage but doesn't know how to "get in the game.") *Having a hard time, huh? This is our first playdate here! Can I sit with you guys and play for a sec? I love this game, actually. Can you both show me how it works?*

WHEN KIDS DON'T WANT TO TALK

Some kids do not like being touched when they're upset. Kids with more introverted personalities may not want to talk, initially, either. In that case, find creative ways to help keep communication open. Put a notebook and a marker next to your child when he's sequestered himself in his room, upset at you or someone else. You don't even have to say anything, just set it down and walk away. If your child can read, then write at the top of the page, *I see you're upset. Can you write to me about what happened?* If he can't read yet, then draw something on the paper and slide it next to him. You may be surprised what he writes or draws back to you. Keep it going back and forth without talking.

Feelings are complex, and sometimes "I'm sad" or "I'm frustrated" isn't really capturing the whole picture. You can help your child make sense of multilayered feelings:

Parent: *How are you feeling about starting school?*

Child: *A little bit scared, and a little bit fun.*

Parent: *Got it. What does the scared part feel like?*

Child: *Like I don't know what will happen and I might not do it right.*

Parent: *Ah, okay. And the fun part feels like . . . ?*

Child: *Like I'm excited to see it, because it's new.*

Hold Off on Arguing, Teaching, and Expecting Apologies

When your child is emotionally flooded—for example, your toddler hit her brother and has collapsed on the ground kicking and screaming, your preschooler is yelling "I hate you, I'm not going!" and is hiding under a chair, or your child slams the door furiously and won't speak—this is not the time to talk about the rules, teach, or explain. Information is not going to be received or integrated. In this mode, your child's emotional brain has overwhelmed him and the logical thinking brain is not in charge.

Parents often feel an irresistible urge to yell out the limit or rule, repeatedly explain what the child did wrong, and expect apologies. This does not help. This is not the time to give a lot of information, beyond attuning and simply stating a limit or reality. Let it go for now. When everyone is calm (even if it's the next day), this is the time to circle back and teach.

Limit Set

After you've attuned, if there is a limit or reality that applies to the situation, state it, along with a brief reason. For example,

This is not snack time. We're leaving some time before dinner with no food, so bellies get hungry and we can enjoy dinner. (limit)

We'll have to bake cookies another time because we don't have brown sugar. (reality)

It's time for your piano lesson, so we have to leave now. (limit)

We're leaving the playground now because it's getting dark. (limit)

My keys are only for me to use. They are not toys. (limit)

We don't have time to go to the park because we've got dinner, homework, and reading time to fit in this evening. (limit)

We are getting in the car now because if we don't, we will be late for school. (limit)

I already cut your food into bites and I can't put it back together. (reality)

The store is closed for the day. The sign on the door says they close at four o'clock. (reality)

I don't have Alex's parents' phone number so I can't make a play-date for you right now. (reality)

Limit-Setting Tool #1:
Make a Direct, Neutral Statement

Make your limit clear and factual. When you're stating a limit or reality, beware of these pitfalls:

Avoid asking a question like *How many times do I have to tell you?* or *Why are you . . . ?* or *Don't you know you can't . . . ?*

Avoid using a harsh tone. Instead, keep your voice calm and in-formative. Kids are geared to explore the world and check things out. They don't care what's dirty, dangerous, or off-limits. It can feel like a constant battle between us and them, but they are meant to test things and, depending on a child's temperament, it might take one hundred times of testing a limit or hearing a rule before each of the "experiments" is over.

Avoid just saying a curt "no!" (Read "Instead of 'No'" on page 42.) More helpful words to use are ones like these:

The keys are not for you; they're only for me to use.

You may not touch the cord. It's dangerous.

Pulling hair isn't okay, because it hurts.

Limit-Setting Tool #2:
Say What You DO Want or What Your Child CAN Do

Let your child know what you *are* asking of him, or what the reality is (not just what's off-limits).

We only put our bottoms or knees on chairs.

Daddy's glasses are for Daddy to wear so he can see!

Doggie's water is only for her to touch.

We close the door after good night, so your room is quiet while you sleep.

In the store, we only pick up the food on our grocery list.

You can have more to eat in the morning.

Tomorrow you will have TV time again.

ATTITUDE AND EYE ROLLING

What can you do if your third-grader rolls his eyes, snaps at you, or talks to you in a rude way? No one wants to feel walked all over or disrespected, but rather than immediately correcting or dwelling on the tip of the iceberg, try a response, in a calm tone, that lets your child try again in a more appropriate way:

It's hard for me to hear your words when you're using that voice. It's distracting me from what you're trying to tell me.

What are you saying to me with your eyes? You didn't like what I just said?

I see your eyes. Are you telling me you want space?

Can you give me that information in a different way? It's easier for me to help you if I understand.

It's hard to work with you when you have that voice. Tell me in a direct way what you want, not what you don't want.

Limit-Setting Tool #3:
Don't Cave

It's tempting to cave and change your limit to make difficult feelings go away, but try not to do this. You can be clear and follow through with your limits, while still being kind.

Our client Amy had an especially hard time holding a limit. Her daughter soon learned that if she begged and pleaded for something in the store, her mom would, after a lengthy negotiation, buy it for her. We uncovered that Amy was worried her daughter wouldn't feel loved, or wouldn't like her, if she held a limit firmly. Eventually, she saw the opposite was true and that her daughter felt safer, less anxious, and closer to her when Amy *was* able to hold a limit firmly and kindly.

Limit-Setting Tool #4:
Reasonable Versus Rigid

We want you to be consistent with limits, not unreasonable or rigid. Parents often ask us if it's okay to negotiate or change your mind when your child has a different plan. The short answer is that, yes, of course it's okay. You shouldn't cave if you deem a limit to be important, or because you simply don't like hearing your child's reaction. Then again, as the parent, you have the ability to change your mind. Especially as your child grows and takes on more responsibility and independence, listen to his ideas and find common ground. As he gets older, he's more likely to have strong opinions and plans that you do want to honor. You'll see more on page 213 about brainstorming and negotiating.

If you decide in the moment that changing your mind and going with your child's desire is possible, without derailing the schedule or breaking a family rule, then you may just decide it's worth it to change directions. You might know your child well enough to see that if you fulfill his wish in the moment, he'll feel satisfied and you'll be able to move on with the day feeling good, rather than digging in for a power struggle just because you've set a limit. If you do decide to do this, own your change of mind rather than just throwing in the towel and feeling resentful. There's a big difference between making a conscious decision to change course and resentfully caving—and our kids pick up on that difference.

You know what, I hear what you're saying and I've changed my mind.

Problem Solve

Now that you've attuned and set a limit, help your child figure out what she *can* do. In the problem-solving step, you're helping her fulfill her intentions in an acceptable way or solve a dilemma. Using some of the examples from earlier in the chapter, here are problem-solving ideas.

Child: *I don't want to go to school!*

Don't feel like it this morning, huh? You'd rather hang out at home. I remember telling Grandma the same thing when I was in kindergarten. I think I wanted to stay in my pj's and eat pancakes, is that about right (attune)? *Okay, well, it's a school day so we are going* (limit). *Could we do something, though? Let's talk more about a pancakes and pj's party idea while we get out to the car. I think Saturday is a good day for that* (problem solve).

This is not snack time. We're leaving some no-food time before dinner, so bellies get hungry and we can enjoy our meal (limit). *Let's see, here are some markers so you could draw the menu for tonight. Or do you want to help me cook? I could use help pouring pasta in this bowl and stirring it* (problem solve).

We'll have to bake cookies another time because we don't have brown sugar (reality). *Let's mark that on our family list to buy brown sugar. Hey, could you show me how you'd do that recipe in your play kitchen* (problem solve)?

We're leaving the playground now because it's getting dark (limit). *Should we hold hands and skip as fast as we can? I bet we can beat our world record. Or, Daddy will gently carry you out of the park* (follow-through choice).

My keys are only for me to use; they are not toys (limit). *I'll put them back in my bag. Look at these sweet little hands, let's play patty-cake with them* (problem solve)!

I already cut your food into bites and I can't put it back together (reality). *Hey, can you count those bites? Did I make them into five bites or more, I don't remember* (problem solve).

The store is closed for the day. The sign on the door says they close at four o'clock (reality). *While we walk, can you tell me what you wanted to look for in there so we remember for next time* (problem solve)?

I don't have Alex's parents' phone number so I can't make a play-date for you right now (reality). *I'll ask your teacher tomorrow for a roster so I have all the parents' phone numbers* (problem solve).

FROM JULIE: SMILING FROM THE AUDIENCE, JUST BETWEEN US!

When my son was in the first grade, he told me his tummy was hurting on the morning of a school performance. He had eaten breakfast and seemed just fine until it was time to go to school. Knowing him as I did, I was pretty sure he was anxious about the performance. Time was short and I had to get ready for work. I was so tempted to just tell him I didn't believe his tummy really hurt and that he had to go to school anyway. But instead, I took a deep breath and asked him to tell me about the performance. He finally told me that he didn't want to do it. Mind you, this was a hundred kids all singing the same song. He would have been almost invisible, but to him it was terrifying. I told him that I understood how scary it felt to get up in front of everyone and sing the song (attune step). I told him that he did have to go to school because he wasn't really sick and that's just the rule (limit-setting step). I asked him what would help and he asked if I would stay with him until we told his teacher he didn't want to perform (problem-solving step). As we drove to school, he began to explore the idea of going ahead with the performance. I suggested that he didn't have to sing, he could just move his lips and pretend to sing. No one would know. It was like our little secret. I'll never forget him up there with all those kids, moving his lips and giving me a knowing little smile. He felt cared about and good about himself because I was able to understand his big feelings and help him find a solution. It seemed like such a small thing, but to him it was big.

Problem-Solving Tool #1:
Propose "Here's What You Can Do"

What does your child want and how can you find an acceptable alternative? If she wants to use the butcher knife, can you offer her a safe plastic knife? If she wants to have mac 'n' cheese for dinner, can you ask her to draw a picture of it on the calendar for later in the week? If she's having a hard time separating from you, can you offer a way to "see each other" after you leave (each of you taking a photo with you to look at while you're apart)?

Problem-Solving Tool #2:
Employ the "Bumbling Parent"

Remember the head-scratching parent from chapter 1? Try to adopt a tone of voice that says "Hmm, let's see. We're in this together and we have to figure it out." As if you're genuinely open to what the best way forward might be. You don't necessarily have all the answers.

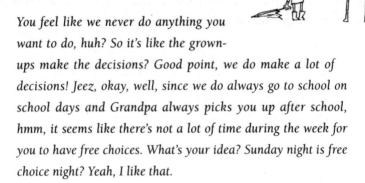

> *You feel like we never do anything you want to do, huh? So it's like the grownups make the decisions? Good point, we do make a lot of decisions! Jeez, okay, well, since we do always go to school on school days and Grandpa always picks you up after school, hmm, it seems like there's not a lot of time during the week for you to have free choices. What's your idea? Sunday night is free choice night? Yeah, I like that.*

Problem-Solving Tool #3:
Use Humor or Say Something Unexpected

This helps you shift the energy and lift your child (and you) out of a tricky situation. For example, one day, Heather's daughter wanted to take a bath in the morning before preschool, but there wasn't enough time. "I'm cold, though! I need a bath, I'm freezing!" her daughter said. "Hmm, yeah, I can see you're chilly. There's not enough time for a bath before school, so let's see . . ." When her daughter started to whine and get upset, Heather said, "Ooh, wait, do you have a snowsuit you could put on? Yeah, we definitely need a snowsuit right now, asap." Her daughter laughed and joined in. While they kept joking and one-upping each other with the layers of cold-weather clothing they should put on, Heather led her daughter to her bedroom to get dressed and keep moving through the routine.

We know it can be challenging, but dig deep to find your humor, even when you're frustrated. Sometimes just one funny sentence can pay off in a huge way when it avoids a spiral of tension and escalation. Unexpected phrases and small creative stories can really change the tone quickly. Take another example that helped Heather's daughter get started one morning:

> *You really don't want to get out of bed this morning, you're so cozy. You're like a cocoon. Here, let me wrap you up in your blanket. I'm just going to scoop you up, but this little butterfly isn't ready to come out of the cocoon. Everyone just give her space for a sec. The butterfly needs to rest on the couch wrapped up. Wait, I think I see a wing popping out . . .*

Problem-Solving Tool #4:
Move Your Body; Change the Scene

Talking is only one way to problem solve. Research indicates that we're more creative and better at problem solving when we move. As you read the following ideas, you'll most likely think "What? No, my child would not like that" for some, and "Oh yeah, I can see that would work" for others. If you recognize some of these from the attune step, it's true, there is overlap in how you use some of these techniques (to attune or problem solve).

Snuggle or wrestle. This really depends on the child and the moment—sometimes kids don't want to talk, they just want physical contact from their most trusted person. Some kids will accept being hugged when they're upset, and it can calm and organize big feelings. Hugging a pillow or stuffed animal can also help when they're not quite ready for a hug from you.

FROM HEATHER: THE GOOD OLD THROW-THEM-ON-THE-BED TECHNIQUE

When my son was in preschool, sometimes if he was having a withdrawn moment and I could tell he wanted to get something out, but he wasn't interested in talking yet, I would make eye contact with him, give him a knowing smile, scoop him up, toss him on the bed, and wrestle with him. I knew sitting down to talk wasn't always the best way to start. I still do it with him at age nine (although, yes, it's harder to throw him, and I'm also likely to lose a wrestling match). Or, if he's on the couch, I just go and sit on him! Usually we both start laughing. Sometimes then I'll move next to him and rub his feet while we talk, if he feels like it.

Walk, skip, dance. Moving helps with managing emotions, improving focus, and learning. Think about how you can use movement in the problem-solving step in a way that's relevant to the initial dilemma or as you're coming up with the solution.

Let's skip out of the park.

Want to walk down the sidewalk while we figure out what to do?

Let's put on music and dance out our feelings!

I'm gonna change that wet diaper while you're crawling (or standing).

How many times can we run around the block?

I want to play catch with you while we talk about this.

Turn them upside down. Yes, upside down! Turning upside down shifts our perspective, and can calm the nervous system. Depending on your child's age, you can turn her upside down or teach her how to do a headstand or hang her head backward over the edge of the sofa. Always let her know, and get her buy-in before you move her body. Of course, you can practice your headstand or handstand too when you're having big feelings or just to join in. Now, if only we could change diapers upside down.

Here, kick your legs up into a handstand. It helps you come up with ideas.

Change the scene. Changing the environment moves your child's focus away from whatever is causing the distress. Remember not to start with this, because it will feel dismissive. Once you've attuned and set a limit if needed, here are some ideas for changing the scene:

I'm going to put my phone in my bag.

As soon as the nurse is done with your shots, we'll walk down the hall to the fish tank.

Let's take a walk while we're waiting for our food to come.

In some cases, the problem-solving step may be to move to calm down, as described on page 133.

Especially if your child is in full tantrum mode or inconsolable, you may need to abandon your original plan. This may be the classic "parent left a full shopping cart at the grocery store." Sometimes our best-laid plans don't work out and that's okay. It's more important that our kids know we're there to help them when they need us. It's hard to shift gears like that, especially if it's something you need to do (get food for dinner) or want to do (spend time with friends). But if your child is overloaded, then as long as you've attuned and held a limit, packing it in and going home can be the best choice.

Problem-Solving Tool #5:
Use a Follow-Through Choice

This is an important tool to have in your back pocket, for those moments when you feel stuck and your child still is not moving or complying. The follow-through is phrased as a choice, but it lets him know that the outcome will ultimately be the same, whether he is on board or not. You'd prefer for him to take ownership, but you will help him get there if he does not. For example,

You can hit the off button, or I can do it for you.

Do you want to put the lovey back in the crib, or I can help you do that.

You can climb in the stroller, or I can lift you in.

Let your child know if you're going to pick him up or move him,

Okay, I see it's hard to choose, I'm going to gently take the lovey from your hands and put it back.

It looks like it's hard for you to get in the stroller. I'm going to pick you up and put you in.

Problem-Solving Tool #6:
Something Like This Happened to Me

Kids often get really curious about our stories if we tell them in the right moments. If they seem stuck, taking the focus off them momentarily can also make them feel more open and creative about problem solving. We expect kids to share their feelings and experiences with us, but sometimes we forget that's a two-way street. Share something about your day or an obstacle you faced and overcame. This isn't an invitation to shift the focus to you or worry your child with your problems (don't talk about stressful topics like money troubles), but being transparent about issues you've had with, for example, not making the team, or having a friend say something mean, can help if you give this information occasionally and in an age-appropriate way. Your goal is to open conversation, and sometimes talking about a person other than themselves helps kids problem solve.

For example, a mom recently told us her daughter wouldn't perform in her jazz concert, despite having been really excited about it. She had stage fright, but later didn't want to talk about it. "Did you ever have stage fright as a kid?" we asked the mom. "Oh yes, big time!" she said. "So you can empathize with your daughter? She may be interested to know about that." The mom had never considered that route. Later she told us she opened a conversation by saying,

> *You were excited about the show, but then you felt like you didn't want to do it? It actually made me remember . . . did you know Mommy had the same feeling when I was your age? I was in a ballet performance but when it was time to go on stage my body froze up and I really didn't want to! It made me nervous. Is that how you were feeling?*

Heather had a similar conversation with her three-year-old daughter, who wanted desperately to wear her tutu to preschool and was furious that she couldn't. Heather said,

> *You're upset because you really want to wear that tutu. It's disappointing. Costumes are for wearing at home, not at school. For school we wear clothes that let us run, jump, climb, and get dirty. (Pause.) You know, I remember one time I wanted to wear this Wonder Woman outfit to preschool and Nana said I couldn't. I was so mad! I was really looking forward to wearing it and I had planned out all the spins and moves I was going to do when I got to school. (Pause.) I had even picked it out and put it by my bed so I'd remember.*

In the case of the dance performance, the mom asked her daughter what she (the mom) could have done to feel brave. They came up with some ideas that the mom as a kid could have used and the daughter in the future could try for the next performance. In the case of Heather's daughter, they picked out a comfortable but twirly skirt for the day and hung the tutu on the doorknob with a note on it saying, *Put me on for playdate with Mila after school!*

EXAMPLE: WHEN IT WORKS FOR ONE CHILD BUT NOT THE OTHER

A mom of two told us that problem solving with her son was pretty smooth. For example, if he wanted a toy in a store she could say, *I know, looks cool. Remember, it's a looking day, not a buying day. Should we put that on our list for later?* He'd be disappointed, but he'd understand and he could recover his good spirits. Her daughter was more opinionated and had bigger feelings, and the same exact techniques didn't land the same way—she'd sit down on the floor in protest. We worked out that, for the daughter, Mom had to remind her before going in the store, empathize more emphatically with her by getting on her level and really letting her know she was understood, and also have a firmer, more decisive tone with her to let her know the limit was set. Sometimes she had to add a follow-through choice to the problem-solving step by saying, *We're leaving the store now. Do you want to walk out holding my hand, or should I help your body out?* and then carry her out of the store. In other words, the mom had to have more energy and creativity to help her daughter, and she also had to be okay with her daughter being stubborn or upset, even after all of that work.

Repair and Circle Back

Repair

There will inevitably be moments when you cringe at something you've said (even as it's on the way out of your mouth), or when you lie in bed at night and think how you should have or could have responded better. Remember that the skill of repair (page 52) is very important. Repair is always there for you if you need it. It's a great message to send your kids that you're not perfect, that you acknowledge what happened, that you're not trying to sweep it under the rug, and that you'll help make sense of it together.

Circle Back

You can always check in with your child later in the day, or the next day, about a difficult moment that happened earlier. This will help her brain create a story and make sense of it. Here's how you might circle back with our earlier example:

> **Parent:** *How are you feeling about starting school?*
>
> **Child:** *A little bit scared, and a little bit fun.*
>
> **Parent:** *Got it. What does the scared part feel like?*
>
> **Child:** *Like I don't know what will happen and I might not do it right.*
>
> **Parent:** *Ah, okay. And the fun part feels like . . . ?*
>
> **Child:** *Like I'm excited to see it, because it's new.*

Later that day,

Parent: *I remember you were feeling scared, and also like you would have fun today. What was it like in the end?*

Child: *It was fun!*

Parent: *Oh yeah? So the fun part really happened?*

Child: *Yes. It was easy!*

Parent: *I'm thinking about that scared part you were mentioning. I wonder, what would you tell your scared part now?*

Child: *Don't worry, it's going to be okay and it'll be fun.*

Scripts and Conversations

You'll notice that some scenarios don't call for a limit-setting step, and that some will be helped by adding a safety step or preparation step. Read these scripts to help you understand how ALP works with difficult feelings. Once you get the hang of it, you'll be able to apply the steps to many different scenarios, use your own words, and sometimes change the order of the steps.

Scripts

Baby

Laying a foundation of open, empathic communication with your baby is invaluable. If you practice this style of talking it becomes second nature. Babies understand more than we think.

SCENARIO: *You're going to change your baby's diaper and he starts to cry.*

PREPARE	ATTUNE	LIMIT SET	PROBLEM SOLVE
I'm gonna lift you up and change your diaper.	I hear ya, you don't feel like lying down and doing a diaper change right now.	I have to change your diaper because it's time.	I'll do it super quick, and you can hold the wipes (or this empty box).

SCENARIO: *Your baby is crying because she can't play with your phone.*

ATTUNE	LIMIT SET	PROBLEM SOLVE
You're sad, I know—my phone looks really interesting, doesn't it!	Phones are for big people. I need to keep my phone in my bag.	Let's find you something with buttons that's fun to play with. I'll put my phone away.

SCENARIO: *You're putting your baby in the car seat and she arches her back and starts to cry.*

PREPARE	ATTUNE	LIMIT SET	PROBLEM SOLVE
In two minutes we're going to get in the car.	You are angry. You don't want to get in your car seat. I know.	We have to drive to pick up your brother, so I do have to get you in now.	Let's get in a cozy position. *(Hold your baby's body in a seated position while you're carrying her.)* And we'll sing a silly song while I put you in.

SCENARIO: *Your baby is climbing up a bookshelf and it's dangerous.*

SAFETY STEP	ATTUNE	LIMIT SET	PROBLEM SOLVE
I'm going to move your body now to keep you safe.	I know, you're frustrated. It looks fun and you wish you could do it.	Bookshelves aren't for climbing. It's dangerous to climb on this because you could fall.	Let's find something we can climb on. Here, we'll put the sofa cushions on the ground and climb over them.

SCENARIO: *Your baby loses it when you take her out of the bathtub. She cries and kicks and squirms.*

ATTUNE	LIMIT SET	PROBLEM SOLVE
You weren't ready to get out of the tub!	I had to take you out because it's time to put pj's on and read books now.	Can I wrap you in your towel like a burrito? Let's see, I think there's a bean burrito for sale here...

SCENARIO: *You hand your baby to someone else and he starts to cry.**

PREPARE	ATTUNE	PROBLEM SOLVE
Let's say hi and give you a chance to remember Aunt Mary before she holds you. Wanna see if she knows how to play peek-a-boo? *(Play for a few minutes.)* Okay, I'll pass you to her for a bit.	Oh, you weren't ready. You wanted to stay with me and that made you feel a little worried, huh?	I'll take you back and we can try again some other time. Should we show Aunt Mary some of your favorite books?

* No limit setting is needed in this scenario.

Toddler/Preschooler

SCENARIO: *Your toddler has grabbed something in the grocery store, and you're telling her she can't have it. In this scenario, your ALP steps go fairly smoothly. (In the next scenario, you need to use additional steps).*

PREPARE	ATTUNE	LIMIT SET	PROBLEM SOLVE
We're going into the store now. I just want to give you some information about it—today we're just buying food for dinner.	I hear you. You really want that stuffed animal. It looks cute.	We're not buying it today because we're just getting what we need for our meals.	Do you want to put it back or should I carry it like a baby back to the shelf? (*Child puts back the animal.*)

SCENARIO: *Your toddler has grabbed something in the grocery store, and you're telling her she can't have it. In this scenario, you need to use a calm-down and follow-through choice.*

PREPARE	ATTUNE	LIMIT SET	PROBLEM SOLVE
We're going into the store now. I just want to give you some information about it—today we're just buying food for dinner.	I hear you. You really want that stuffed animal. It looks cute.	We're not buying it today because we're just getting what we need for our meals.	Do you want to put it back or should I carry it like a baby back to the shelf? (*Child starts to yell.*) It looks like it's hard to choose, so I'm going to put it back (follow-through step). (*Child starts screaming.*) I'm going to gently move your body out of the store where it's quiet (*calm-down step: Pick her up, as gently as possible, and walk outside. Take some deep breaths.*)

SCENARIO: *You need to leave the park and your toddler doesn't want to.*

PREPARE	ATTUNE	LIMIT SET	PROBLEM SOLVE
We're going to leave soon. Do your last few swings!	You don't want to go—I know it's hard to leave when you're swinging that high and having fun.	We need to leave because Daddy called and said dinner is ready now.	We could do "follow the leader" out, or I could fly you like an airplane. *(Pause.)* Hard to leave, huh? Okay, I'm going to help you. I'm going to lift you up *(follow-through step)*.

If your child is still crying when you get in the car, you can repeat one or more of your steps as you're driving home. Say something empathic once or twice, like "I know you were sad to leave." As he calms down, start singing his favorite song, or try another problem-solving step.

SCENARIO: *You're at the breakfast table and your toddler cries because the egg is cooked the wrong way. In this scenario you are not going to cook another egg or offer other food choices.*

PREPARE	ATTUNE	LIMIT SET	PROBLEM SOLVE
I'm making toast and eggs. Do you want fried, scrambled, or sunny-side up? *(Child doesn't answer, or changes her mind after you serve it.)*	Oh, wow, this wasn't the egg you had in mind? You look pretty mad about this egg.	I've already cooked the egg, so this is the choice for this meal. You can eat as much of it as you want, or leave it on your plate.	Do you want to put some pepper on it? *(Or)* Could you draw me a quick picture of scrambled eggs? I'll put that Post-it Note on the calendar for tomorrow.

If your child is still crying at the table and is disrupting other people: "I hear how frustrated you are. We can't really yell or cry loudly at the table because it's interrupting other people. I'll move you to a calm-down space where we can take some deep breaths together."

SCENARIO: *You're playing at a friend's house and it's time to go home. Your toddler always wants to take one of her friend's toys when she leaves.*

PREPARE	ATTUNE	LIMIT SET	PROBLEM SOLVE
We're going to go home in five minutes—remember it was hard to say good-bye to Diego's toys last time? Let's get ready to wave good-bye to them.	I understand. It's really hard to leave Diego's cool toys here.	We have to leave his toys here because they belong to him.	Let's say, "See you next time, toys," and blow them kisses as we walk away. Let's blow a kiss to Diego too!

School-Age Child

SCENARIO: *Your daughter is sad about the outcome of a baseball game.*

ATTUNE	REALITY	PROBLEM SOLVE
You're sad about how that game ended up today?	The other team won and you didn't get on base. Your team is working hard and still coming together.	If there was one thing you wanted to work on in practice this week, what would it be?

SCENARIO: *Your child is sick and really upset about missing a birthday party.*

ATTUNE	LIMIT SET	PROBLEM SOLVE
It's hard, I know you wanted to go to that party. You're disappointed.	We're going to stay home to let your body rest. And it's important not to get other people sick too.	Should we plan a special playdate with your friend to celebrate?

Conversations

Your Son Comes Home and Says He's Terrible at Basketball.

It was a frustrating game, huh?

Yeah, I suck. (Hangs head.)

You felt like you kept trying and it wasn't quite clicking.

(Nods but doesn't talk.)

I see. Sounds discouraging. (Pause. Resist saying things like, "You're great! It'll be better next time. Don't get so down on yourself!")

I never got a single basket. I make them in practice, but I never even took a shot today.

You're making baskets at practice. Games are different, though?

Yeah. Danny was hogging the ball. It's like I have to yell super loud for a pass or I never get the ball.

You feel like it takes yelling really really loud, to even just get a chance to have the ball and take a shot.

Yeah.

Let me know if you want to head to the park and practice that. I could be Danny and you could get open and yell really loud to me.

Your Daughter Is Worried about a Piano Recital Later that Day.

I'm worried about the recital.

You're not sure about it? What are you worried will happen?

I keep thinking about messing up.

I totally understand that feeling. Sure, everyone messes up sometimes. What's your plan? What did your teacher say you should do if you messed up?

Start over at the beginning.

Gotcha. So you have a plan for that. I'll be there—do you want to smile at each other if it happens? I've got your back.

Yes.

Your Son Was Reprimanded by His Teacher for Talking Too Much During Class.

My teacher is so stupid. I hate her.

I hear ya. Doesn't feel good to be called out like that.

Lots of other kids were talking too; it wasn't only me.

It felt like she singled you out.

Yes.

It's no fun to feel like you're the only one in trouble. Hm, well, since we know the rules at school are what they are, any ideas for what to do tomorrow?

Stay home?

Ha! Good one. Maybe you could find a way to remind yourself to save the talking for recess.

I guess I could move a little away from my friends so I don't get tempted into talking.

That's a great idea.

Your Daughter's Feelings Were Hurt by a
Friend at School.

Maya said I'm not her friend anymore.

Oh, huh . . . (Pause to see if she wants to add anything before you guide the conversation.) *Not friends anymore?*

Yeah.

And what was it like when she said that?

Sad.

Yeah, I can see why that would make you feel sad. What else happened?

She was playing with Fiona and they said I couldn't play with them.

They were in a game that you wanted to join, but they had a different plan? What do you think she meant by not being her friend?

She wanted to play with Fiona instead.

Got it, so she wanted time with Fiona. Do you ever wonder what people really mean when they say they're not your friend? To me, sometimes it means they want space or want to play with someone else for a bit. Have you ever felt that way, like you're really into playing with one friend, and you'll see the other friend later?

FROM HEATHER: EXPLORING FEELINGS WITHOUT SOLVING OR TEACHING

I noticed my daughter hid behind my legs when we got to preschool in the morning. Teachers would say hi and try to talk to her, but she wouldn't say anything or look at them. I thought I'd open the conversation with my daughter to help shed some light on it. My goal was just to understand her and give her a chance to talk about it. Walking to school one morning I said, *I noticed something when I dropped you off at school. I noticed that all the teachers seem very friendly and like they want to say hi and talk to you. And I noticed that you look the other way and don't say anything.*

She nodded.

What's going on for you when that happens?

I'm not ready yet.

Oh, I see. You're not really ready to start talking. You're still warming up.

Yes.

Got it. So it feels like . . .

Like I need more time.

I see. (I waited for a bit and continued.) *I actually remember that when Nana took me somewhere and I'd just arrived and people were talking to me, I'd hide behind her legs!*

Really? Why?

I guess I wasn't ready yet.

Like you weren't ready to look at them or talk yet. You needed more time.

Yes.

CHAPTER FOUR

Hitting, Pushing, Biting, and Other Physical Behaviors

If your child is going to develop a healthy personal-
ity . . . she must learn how to test reality, regulate her
impulses, stabilize her moods, integrate her feelings
and actions, focus her concentration, and plan.

—Stanley Greenspan, MD

Aaron was a lovely dad who was perplexed by his suddenly aggressive toddler. Two-and-a-half-year-old Ella had started hitting him when she didn't get what she wanted. It was usually over something seemingly insignificant, like having to get out of the tub or getting the Sleeping Beauty towel instead of the Cinderella one. She had never done this before, and it really worried him. Aaron would sternly say, "No hitting. Stop that!" As Ella continued to hit, Aaron quickly escalated to anger and scolding. "I said no! Why are you doing that? How many times do I have to tell you to stop hitting?" Ella would lose control and start kicking and screaming. He put her in time-out, but it didn't seem to work. They were both frustrated and angry. He came to us worried he'd gotten off track, and wondering what to do to get through to her and make her stop.

Later in this chapter we'll discuss how Aaron used ALP to solve Ella's physical aggression, but as many parents know, this dilemma is a common one: Many babies and young kids express themselves physically when they're upset, excited, overwhelmed, or trying to get someone's attention. These behaviors can appear in the form of hitting, biting, pushing, pulling hair, pinching, and kicking, starting as young as eight to ten months of age.

Contrary to what you might think, hitting and biting is normal for babies and toddlers, so if your child does this, try not to worry. With the ALP steps in this chapter, you can make a plan and be ready for what to do and say. The key is to see these physical behaviors as the tip of the iceberg and figure out what's underneath (attune), to be very clear that hurting other people's bodies is not okay (limit set), and to help kids find other ways to express themselves (problem solve). There is always a reason our little ones do what they do, and we can be empathic while we also help them solve their dilemmas. Being curious about what is going on in your child's inner mental world is the key to knowing how to respond in a way that is connected, consistent, and collaborative.

For some kids, learning not to hit takes time. If your toddler is acting out in a physical way, think of your job as helping him along in a process—soon his brain will take over the job of making better choices. You may have to respond quickly and repeatedly, over and over, until this happens.

Why Do Little Kids Hit?

Let's talk about the reasons that kids hit, push, or bite. This will help you understand and maybe even address the cause. Do a quick scan to see if you can guess why your toddler might be hitting (also see further explanations in the pages that follow). Children may be:

- Sleep deprived (We see this a lot!)
- Overstimulated (too loud, too hot, too much sensory input)
- Understimulated (bored, lonely)
- Hungry
- Trying to connect or express something

- Testing the world and people's reactions
- Frustrated—unable to get needs met
- Unable to do what they see others doing
- Overwhelmed by excited, happy emotions

My child hits when:

_____

_____

Sometimes kids hit because they feel threatened and backed into a corner—it's their fight-or-flight reaction. Other times, it's anger or aggression. Can you add anything to the list above?

Hitting and other physical behaviors are developmentally normal, for these reasons:

Little kids test and experiment. Kids learn about the world by trying behaviors and seeing reactions. The problem is that this natural process of testing often conflicts with social rules and ways we want them to behave. It doesn't mean we should allow kids to hit; it means we need to be right there to guide them to communicate clearly with words, rather than physical acts. For some kids, this can take time, because the developing brain has strong feelings and desires, but not so much self-regulation and impulse control. This makes it easier for kids to become emotionally flooded.

If kids aren't allowed to express their feelings, those feelings will come out in other ways. Our kids' emotions need a place to go. This is why we listen, allow them to express themselves, and give them the sense that all feelings are welcome. If we're solely focused on controlling and punishing, without looking at the feelings and needs underneath, our kids don't have an emotional outlet. When this happens, those emotions can be *externalized* (see page 26), which may take the form of hitting and other physical behaviors. Some kids may *internalize* their feelings, meaning that the child becomes reticent, withdrawn, anxious, or depressed.

Developmental gaps. Babies and toddlers have very normal but profound gaps in language and motor skills that lead to intense frustration and struggle. First, their receptive language (ability to understand what they hear) is way ahead of their expressive language (ability to speak), which is a huge source of confusion and unhappiness as they struggle to communicate without words. Second, they are able to see what older kids and adults are able to do physically (climb the ladder to the slide, reach the cookies on the counter, run around the park) that they are not able to do. Both of these lead to frustration and struggle, which is part of a natural developmental process. The desire to do an activity you can't do yet, or say something you can't quite express, is motivating and it's a normal, even good, part of learning.

Your child is trying to tell you something. Kids sometimes act in big ways to get our attention. If the parent is distracted, the day is overscheduled, the parents' relationship is tense, or something similar, kids do things to stop us and get us to engage. For some kids, acting out in these ways is the only way they feel they get their parents' undivided attention.

Your child is imitating. Little kids can imitate or try out what they see and feel at home or out in the world. If there is yelling, spanking, or hostility at home or school, they are more likely to hit, push, or bite in a difficult moment.

HOW TO KNOW WHEN TO ASK FOR HELP

Hitting and biting are normal for some toddlers and become less common around age four. If you're concerned, or if your child's teacher is concerned, it's always good to consult with a professional. A pattern of hitting or biting that lasts can be a sign of another developmental issue and early intervention can make a big difference.

Temperaments are different. Some children are more watchful, thoughtful, and careful. Others have physical impulses closer to the surface and need more time and learning to develop self-control and express what they're feeling with words.

Teaching a rule or set of behaviors can be long and painstaking. Some kids try something once (or even learn from watching others), file that lesson away, and move on. Others conduct repeated experiments until they're satisfied with the results and internalize the lesson. It can feel very frustrating to parents to have to repeat themselves over and over, but some kids need many, many patient repetitions of ALP.

Not enough exercise and outdoor time. Amazingly, research shows that only one in three children is physically active each day, and kids spend a daily average of seven and a half hours in front of screens. Little kids need a lot of time for running, unstructured play, and time outside. Some kids benefit from roughhousing (provided both parties agree) and other kinds of physical play.

Not enough sleep. When we do not sleep enough, the first skills we lose are our emotional control, patience, planning, and creative problem solving. Kids who are chronically under-slept (even by thirty minutes per night) are more likely to have problems with emotional regulation and impulse control. Babies and little kids need eleven to twelve hours of nighttime sleep. On our website thehappysleeper.com, or in our book *The Happy Sleeper*, you'll find detailed recommendations for each age group, including naps and optimal schedules. Healthy sleep is critical to feeling emotionally balanced.

Parents' Knee-Jerk Reactions

Yelling, Scolding, and Punishments

If you look back at the case of Ella hitting her dad over the wrong princess towel, his reaction seems pretty understandable, doesn't it? She would take swings at him for what seemed like the smallest, silliest reasons. The more he scolded her, the worse her behavior got. It was understandably infuriating.

The first step we worked on with him was to change his tone. He thought he needed to be stern to make her stop hitting, but the opposite was true. Scolding escalates and amplifies the tension and it gets you stuck at the tip of the iceberg, which is where Aaron was with Ella. After meeting with us (and our doing a lot of convincing that a reprimanding tone was counterproductive) he used a kind, calm tone with her when she hit instead. This almost instantly shifted the dynamic in a surprising way. You'll see in a moment what he did next.

Remember, your job is to be the steady navigator in a storm of emotions. Resist the impulse to yell or punish, and instead see this as a teaching moment when your child is telling you she needs your help.

Here are two more reactions to avoid.

Do not spank or hit your child. There are many reasons not to spank a child, including:

- Spanking models the exact behavior you want them to stop.
- Spanking creates fear, anger, and shame. This makes kids shut down, so it's impossible for them to take in all the nuances and details of life that you are trying to teach.

- Spanking erodes trust and the sense that you are here to help and guide your kids.
- Occasional spanking, in a moment of uncontrolled anger, can be more harmful, because kids feel a high level of shame and believe that they must be very "bad."

Do not send your child to time-out. It may seem like a logical consequence for hitting, pushing, or biting, but we're going to teach you a better way. When you send your child to time-out in a scolding, punitive manner, he does not spend this time reflecting on his behavior, developing better coping and communication skills, or crafting better responses for next time. Instead, he is isolated and shamed, and usually ends the time-out period feeling embarrassed, defeated, or resentful. Kids who are given a punishment of time-out for hitting or biting are very likely to repeat the behavior. Time-out shuns and isolates a child who needs understanding, teaching, and redirecting. Instead of a time out, use calm down (page 49) if needed.

ALP for Hitting and Other Physical Behaviors

The instinct your young child has to solve his issue physically is absolutely normal. Every time it happens, you have an opportunity to let him know you understand his issue, will consistently hold a limit on his behavior, and will be his helper in learning how to communicate and fulfill his needs in an acceptable way. When you're responding to physical behaviors, here are the steps to use.

ALP FOR PHYSICAL BEHAVIORS

Safety step. Calmly make sure everyone is safe.

Stop. Wait. Be safe.

Attune. Attend to the person who was hurt first. Say what you see. To the person who hit, acknowledge the *feelings or intentions* that are beneath the behavior. Calm down if needed. Wait until she's calm and receptive to problem solve.

You got frustrated, huh?

You hit him and now he's crying. That looks like it really hurt.

You were trying to tell him something . . .

Limit set. Consistently communicate and hold the limit/rule and show that these *behaviors* are never okay. Briefly explain why.

We absolutely do not hit, because it hurts other people.

Problem solve. Prompt your child to check in with the friend who is hurt. Help your child fulfill the intention in an acceptable way. Continue to use calm down, if needed. Use natural consequences.

Let's check in and see if your friend needs an ice pack.

Since you guys have a lot of energy, let's see if you could do a race to the tree!

You're showing me you need to change seats for now.

Safety Step

With physical behaviors, it's important to first ensure everyone's safety. We want to send our kids a clear message that these behaviors are simply never okay. In the safety step, you physically hold the boundary and prevent the hit, bite, or push from happening, or at least from happening again. Depending on the situation you may:

- Put your hand up to block and hold a hitting hand or kicking foot.
- Gently move your child away from you or another person.
- Walk or move your child to a quiet place.

All of the above would be done while communicating that you need to start by keeping everyone safe in a factual, not scolding, "just gotta do it" tone. Say something like,

Stop, wait, be safe.

Pause. We need to be safe.

I'm going to keep everyone safe.

Your feet are hurting me. I'm going to turn you around.

I see that's hurting. I'm going to help your hands stop doing that.

Use your actions to show the child how seriously you're going to take this. If your child is hitting regularly, be ready to respond quickly as much as possible. This means you may have to closely supervise playdates and trail behind your child at the park for a while.

Attune

Now that you've sent a clear message about stepping in when physical behaviors arise, you can attune. Let your child know you understand how he's feeling and what is underneath these physical acts. This is your attune "toolbox"; you can use the ones that fit the situation.

Attune Tool #1: First, Attune to the Child Who Was Hurt

It's the right, natural thing to do to attune first to the person who might be hurt. Attuning to the child who was hurt (whether it's a sibling or a friend) also helps your child connect the dots between what he did and the pain or reaction it caused. This helps build awareness and empathy, and some kids need more explicit teaching to see this over and over before they understand it. Say something like

> *I saw his foot kick you, are you okay?*

> *Can I see your leg? That looked like it hurt. Let me help you up.*

If someone needs soothing or medical attention, provide this first without worrying about who's to blame or exactly what happened. When immediate needs are met, you can use your other steps to gather more information and think about the limit-setting and problem-solving steps.

Attune Tool #2: Say What You See, or What You Don't See

The sportscaster technique. The sportscaster is a great tool to use in conflicts. Rather than taking a side or blaming, just describe what you see. You're like a radio sportscaster giving the play-by-play:

> *You hit him and now he's crying. He looks hurt.*

Jack, you look upset. Jane, you swung your arm at his head.

The investigative reporter technique. Often you don't see, or aren't really paying attention, to the beginnings of a conflict, so you don't really know what happened. This can be a good thing, if you use it properly. Even if you think you know exactly what the conflict is about or it's something that happens a lot, try suspending your assumption.

What happened here? I didn't see it.

I see you're crying and you look frustrated. Can someone fill me in?

When kids get the reputation of being a "problem," it's easy for adults to feed into a cycle by expecting them to misbehave. As much as possible, avoid a tone of "Oh, here we go again. What did you do now?" This contributes to a story of a child who causes problems, and it can make the child more likely to assume this is his identity and follow along with the story. Instead, stay curious and gather the facts.

Attune Tool #3: Attune to Your Child

One you've checked in with the child who's hurt, attune to your child. Needless to say, exuding empathy and understanding toward your child when he is actively hitting or kicking can seem impossible, not to mention indulgent. But take a breath and keep yourself calm. Remember, you are not going to excuse hitting or let it go, but if your child hurts someone, he's telling you he needs your help. Use your iceberg analogy and think, *What's under this behavior? What is he trying to accomplish or figure out?* In a tone that communicates awareness and curiosity, let him know what you think he's feeling in this moment and what led to the physical behaviors. For example:

> *You wanted the ball, I get that.*

> *It's really hard to get out of the tub when you're having fun.*

> *I know you don't want to get into your car seat right now.*

> *Oh, wow, were you trying to say you wanted that toy?*

> *You're trying to tell your friend something, but you're using your hands.*

> *This amusement park is overwhelming, I know. I think we're both feeling like this is too much!*

You don't always have to get it right, but he needs to feel that you're doing your best to understand and empathize. This step may be only one or, at the most, two sentences.

In the case of Ella hitting her dad in the bath, Aaron had been responding to the tip of the iceberg when she hit him. Within a few minutes of talking, he revealed that Ella had a new baby brother. Since the baby's birth, Aaron had been doing Ella's bedtime routine (which mom used to do) and this was usually when the hitting happened. He knew these were all big changes for Ella, but he didn't know what to do with this information to help her stop hitting. We suggested that, instead of starting by correcting her behavior, he speak first to the beneath-the-surface communication. When she hits you, we said, gently block her hands and in a kind tone of voice, say,

It's different. I know. Mommy usually gives you a bath, so this must feel a little strange. You're telling me you don't like this right now. We're figuring it out together.

It sounded so indulgent to Aaron when we suggested it. "But she hit me. Don't I have to teach her that's wrong?" he reacted. We convinced him that if he addressed the underlying communication, while holding the limit, he would be more effective at teaching. She was telling her dad something in the way her two-year-old brain and body were able to in those moments. It was his job as the parent to try to see what was really going on.

The next week he came back to report that he had tried it. The first night, he said a version of what we had suggested, while gently blocking her hands from hitting. She seemed a little taken aback at his calm, empathic tone. The situation didn't escalate, and he felt more in control and positive. She still hit him several times over the next few weeks, but with his calm and steady response, the dynamic rapidly changed. Her hitting stopped, and they were able to enjoy the bedtime routine together. Aaron was relieved. He told us that he had been worried he was failing because his daughter hit, and was so annoyed and anxious to make her stop, he couldn't see what she was trying to tell him. He had to consciously let go of the tip-of-the-iceberg behavior and zero in on what was underneath.

FROM JULIE

I find examples of how empathy can dissolve aggression and conflicts in the most unexpected places sometimes. Recently I caught a scene in an old TV show. Henry Winkler was playing a very timid new sheriff in a Wild West town. Terrified when he was called upon to break up a bar brawl and in the clutches of the brutish villain, he said to the villain, "You seem really upset—what's going on?" The villain proceeded to tell him how his wife had left him. Henry said, "I can understand why that would be upsetting," and the villain broke down in tears, distraught about his predicament. He released Henry from his clutches, as Henry suggested he talk to his wife and tell her he would change his ways. "Will it work?" the villain asked. "Only if she believes you mean it," said Henry. I was struck by the fact that the pivotal point in this Wild West show was the empathic response to a truly difficult (life-threatening) moment.

Limit Set

Say the rule and give a brief reason. Use a matter-of-fact, "well, this is just the way it is" tone.

We don't hit, because it hurts other people.

It's absolutely not okay to hurt another person.

Biting (pushing, kicking, pinching, etc.) is not okay. It hurts people.

I'm going to stop you every time until you learn to stop yourself.

Remember that kids with challenging temperaments need us to state limits firmly, with a confident voice. This doesn't mean yelling, it means having a loud enough voice to be heard, and a serious enough tone to get through. Your child needs to know that you mean it and that you will stop him every single time until he is able to stop himself.

Problem Solve

The problem-solving step with physical behaviors will be to check in, to practice conflict resolution, and to think of creative and helpful ways to solve the problem or address the child's needs.

Problem-Solving Tool #1:
Checking In instead of Saying Sorry

It's normal to want to ask your child to say sorry, but saying sorry can become rote and meaningless. It doesn't give the child a way to help, see what the other person needs, or keep the conversation going. It's even more helpful for your child to say to the injured person,

Are you okay?

Can I help?

Do you need some ice?

Rather than imposing a "say sorry" rule, ask the child who hit to "check in" with the person he hurt and see if he can do anything to help. Say something like,

Check in with Aiden.

Let's check in with Aiden and see if he needs anything.

How can you let Aiden know that you didn't mean to hurt him?

How can we help Aiden feel better?

Come with me. Can you bring this ice pack back to Aiden?

This is your way of scaffolding (page 243) so that kids can practice conflict resolution.

If your child won't say anything or check in with the other person, don't focus too heavily on it. You check in for him, ask how the other person is, and attend to that person's needs. Each time it happens, continue to prompt your child to check in, and assume he will do it. Eventually he will. Don't give up. Checking in is not a punishment. If you need to model it for your child dozens of times before he picks up on it and starts to do it himself, that's okay.

"BUT I DIDN'T DO IT!"

Sometimes one kid will say, *I didn't do it! She fell herself!*

To which we say, *Our job right now is to check in with her because she got hurt.*

Checking in is not a punishment or blame situation, it's a genuine curiosity about whether the other person is okay. So, for the time being, it doesn't matter who did what.

Problem-Solving Tool #2:
Fulfill the Intention

Wonder aloud about other ways your child could accomplish what she was trying to do when she hit. For example,

You didn't want to get into your car seat. Let me find you something fun to hold and you can help get your arms in, while I quickly buckle you.

It's hard when I am making dinner and can't pick you up. How about if I put you in the carrier on my back so you can watch and we can sing songs?

I saw her grab the toy from you. What could you say instead of hitting—"I'm working with that."

Let's see, you were trying to get a turn on the tire swing. How could you let them know with your words that you want to swing next?

You were trying to get into the game. What could you say— "Hey, I want to play too"?

You were angry. What could you do if you're angry instead of hitting? Could you say in loud, clear words, "This is making me mad! Listen to my words!"

GENTLE TOUCH WITH BABIES WORKS!

Little babies can be rough, not because they're trying to hurt others but because they have poor modulation, meaning that a soft, gentle touch on someone's body or a caress of someone's (or a pet's) hair is almost impossible for them. They also don't understand that the rough touch can hurt. We've learned, after many years of Mommy and Me classes, that if parents use ALP to patiently and repeatedly show and teach their babies "gentle touch," in the problem-solving step, the babies do eventually get it. It helps to generalize "gentle touch" as you show them. You say, *I touch your arm gently, I take your hand and touch my face gently and then I take your hand and touch your hair gently, and then we can both touch the dog's fur gently,* and so on. It may seem like a lot to do but the payoff is big as you watch your very young baby learn *how* to touch.

Problem-Solving Tool #3: Solve the Dilemma

What triggers from the list on page 155 seem like they contribute to the physical behaviors? When you used your iceberg analogy in the attune step, you uncovered the root cause, and this can lead you to relevant solutions.

Let's do a fast dance and get our big feelings out.

Let's go home, put our pj's on, and make dinner.

You know what, I really need a snack. Let's sit in the shade and eat something.

I'm going to sit and play with you two. Seems like you need a little help. What are we playing here, cars?

Hand your baby a toy or teether that she *can* bite.

Turn your baby's body around so she can't bite you and give her a deep hug.

Have a sock-throwing party, where you ball up socks and throw them around the room.

Hug a stuffed animal.

Work with Play-Doh.

Sing how you're feeling loudly.

Take your child to calm down (see page 49).

If your child has been hitting or biting people inside or outside the family, make this part of the family meeting agenda. In the meeting you could brainstorm other ways to tell people what you want, what to do if you're upset, breathing techniques, solutions from your iceberg analogy, and more.

Let's talk about our bedtime routine and what time we all go to bed. I realize all of us need to fill up on sleep a little more.

I noticed on the calendar we have a lot going on this week. Let's make sure we have one afternoon of free time and no plan. A day when we get to do whatever comes up.

Problem-Solving Tool #4:
Use Natural Consequences instead of Punishments

In some cases, the logical, safe step is to leave a playdate or the park, or take away a toy that is being used unsafely. This is not a punishment, it's a natural consequence of a child being unsafe. Often kids who are hitting do need to take a break, eat a snack, or change the scene. In a neutral tone, say something like,

You're showing me that you need a break from the park. We're going home and we'll try again tomorrow.

I'm taking the broom now, because you're not being safe with it.

Using ALP on Yourself

ALP is multidirectional. It works from parent to child, parent to parent, and even parent to him- or herself. So later on, in a quiet moment, give yourself a chance to reflect with kindness toward yourself. This will help you be ready for the next time you encounter a difficult moment. If you accept and understand all of *your* feelings, you'll be capable of doing the same for your child.

1. Attuning. When your child hits, bites, or acts out, what thoughts and feelings do you have? Scared that your child is being aggressive? Worried it means you're not an effective parent? Embarrassed about what others will think? Angry because it reminds you of someone or something else? These are all very normal and natural feelings and thoughts to have. If you're aware of them, you will have more freedom to choose what you do next. See more ideas for how to be curious about your own reactions on page 84.

2. Limit setting or stating the reality. Remind yourself of the realities. Acting out physically means your little one needs help soothing, calming down, or learning how to express himself in a nonphysical way. He is not intentionally being bad. He needs you to be on his side and consistently teach and guide him. You are the calm in the storm.

3. Problem solving. Choose and plan out what to do. Get ready to follow the simple steps outlined in this chapter. Every time you remember to approach these moments with empathy *and* consistency, you will be shifting the pattern of your response in a chosen, mindful way as opposed to a reactive, knee-jerk one. It's also fine if you forget sometimes. Go back, repair, and have a "do-over."

Scripts and Conversations

Scripts

Baby

SCENARIO: *Your baby pulls the dog's hair.*

ATTUNE	LIMIT SET	PROBLEM SOLVE
You want to touch Rex. He's fun to play with, huh?	It's not okay to pull his hair, because that hurts him.	Let's use a gentle touch. Let me show you.

Note: Babies learn about the world by touching and experimenting, and they lack modulation in their actions, so pulling hair and even biting aren't necessarily aggressive acts. Your job in these scenarios is to teach your baby (with many patient repetitions) a different way to explore.

SCENARIO: *Your baby bites your arm.*

ATTUNE	LIMIT SET	PROBLEM SOLVE
Your teeth are really bothering you, I can see that.	Biting me is not okay, because it hurts.	I'll give you a cold washcloth or teether that you can bite.

(Or)

You want to be close to me.	It's not okay to bite, because it hurts people.	Let's do some really big hugs!

Note: Babies usually aren't biting out of aggression but because they're teething or because they're craving pressure or physical proximity to us.

SCENARIO: *Your baby hits you because you won't give her your keys.*

SAFETY	ATTUNE	LIMIT SET	PROBLEM SOLVE
I'm going to stop your hands.	You really want my keys!	Hitting is not okay, because it hurts people. Keys are only for Mom or Dad to hold. They're a little sharp.	You can hold this spatula or your red, blue, and green keys instead.

Toddler/Preschooler

SCENARIO: *Your toddler hits a friend who has just taken a toy out of his hand. The child is hurt and starts to cry.*

ATTUNE	LIMIT SET	PROBLEM SOLVE
(Attend to the child who was hit.) I saw that. Are you okay?	We do not hit, because it hurts other people.	*(Address your child.)* Let's ask your friend if he's okay.
(Address your child.) You didn't like it when he took the toy? You were still playing with it.		*(Address the other child.)* Were you trying to ask for a turn with that toy?
Hm, seems like you're both interested in this toy.		*(Play the head-scratching, bumbling parent.)* What could the plan be?

SCENARIO: *Two siblings, a toddler and a child, are playing a card game. The older one starts yelling, "That's not fair, you're breaking the rules!" He takes the cards away and the toddler bites his arm.*

SAFETY STEP	ATTUNE	LIMIT SET	PROBLEM SOLVE
(Swiftly but kindly move the toddler away.)	*(Attend to the bitten child.)* Are you okay? Let me see your arm.	Biting is never okay because it hurts.	Please check in with your brother.
	(Address the toddler.) You got really mad when he took the cards, huh?		Do you guys want to have a snack before playing again?

SCENARIO: *Two kids run to the slide at the same time. They both try to push their way to the front and end up pushing each other, hard.*

ATTUNE	LIMIT SET	PROBLEM SOLVE
Oh, wow. I saw that. You both really want to be first on the slide.	I'm going to stop you from pushing because, as you know, pushing that hard can be dangerous.	Take three deep breaths with me. What's your plan for taking turns on the slide?

School-Age Kid

SCENARIO: *Your child's team lost a soccer game. You see your daughter kick a girl from the winning team.*

ATTUNE	LIMIT SET	PROBLEM SOLVE
I saw you kick her. I know you're really frustrated about not winning the game.	Kicking people is absolutely not okay. It really hurts.	I'll go with you to check in and see if she's okay. Then you can tell me your feelings instead of using your feet to show them.

SCENARIO: *An eight-year-old boy is angry and out of control when his video game playing time is up. He throws a glass, which hits the wall and breaks.*

SAFETY STEP	ATTUNE	LIMIT SET	PROBLEM SOLVE
Stop. Everyone stay where you are. There's broken glass. Is anyone hurt?	I get that it feels terrible to stop your game in the middle.	You may not throw or break things. It's incredibly dangerous. It could really hurt someone, as I'm sure you see.	What do you think we should do now? (*Wait for him to suggest an action, like getting the broom.*) Sounds like a good plan. (*Later, continue.*) I can help you write a list of things that are okay to do when you get angry, like tear up old newspapers or punch pillows. I'm sure you have some good ideas.

Conversations

Two siblings, a child and a toddler, are playing. The child is provoking the toddler, and she gets frustrated and pinches him very hard. In this conversation, the dad uses the sportscaster and looks under the tip of the iceberg, rather than punishing.

Ouch! She just pinched me!

Let me see. Are you okay? (He rubs the child's arm.) *I saw you two playing and then you yelled. What happened?*

He was laughing at me and it was mean! (Starts to cry and is clearly upset by the whole interaction. The dad can see the toddler is feeling overwhelmed.)

Come here, sit on my lap for a second. Can I give you a hug? (The toddler collapses in her dad's lap. To the child, while still touching him too, the dad continues.) *Can you also tell me what happened?*

I was just joking and then she pinched me.

You thought what you were saying was funny, but it looks like she had a different reaction to it. Anything I missed? (Pause) *Is your arm okay?* (He addresses the toddler.) *Pinching hurts—that's not okay to do. In our family we tell each other in clear voices what we want or feel. What could you say instead, if you don't like what he's saying, maybe,"Stop laughing at me right now. I do not like that." Would that work? Let's do one of those dragon breaths we all practiced together at our family meeting. Ready . . .*

CHAPTER FIVE

Listening, Following Directions, and Engaging Cooperation

LEARNING

ALP FOR LISTENING AND COOPERATION

> *Punishments and rewards are not really opposites, but*
> *two sides of the same coin. . . . Neither strategy helps*
> *children to grapple with the question "What kind of*
> *person do I want to be?"*
>
> —Alfie Kohn

One of the biggest sources of frustration for parents is when kids don't listen, they ignore directions, or they disregard a family rule. No doubt you have your own daily stories: your toddler goes stiff as a board when you try to jam her in the stroller; your child moves in slow motion to clean up his room and do homework; or, despite your daily instruction to "be nice to your brother," your daughter still provokes and teases him until they both end up in tears. These are moments when all you want is some control and sanity. You just want your words to *work*.

When we teach ALP for engaging cooperation, parents sometimes wonder if it's realistic. They've read books and articles on being positive and empathic, but they'll tell us that in the heat of the moment, it feels like too much to expect. Or, they worry it will undermine their authority. The consensus among busy, multitasking parents is "It's too much talking. I just need it to happen!"

We get it. We also believe that there is some confusion out there about what it actually means to attune or be empathic. This gets confused with helicoptering, overhelping, permissiveness, or trying to make kids happy all the time. The fact is that it is very possible to attune, collaborate, *and* still be effective. In fact, in this chapter you'll see how *listening to your child* makes him more likely to *listen to you*.

At the same time, keep in mind that blind obedience is not the goal. Over time, we want kids to become independent thinkers and to make good choices and cooperate because it comes from within. That means seeing them as capable, assuming they have good intentions and are trying to navigate the world, explaining the reasons for limits, and giving them enough space to test and learn from experience. Remember that self-discipline comes from *self*, not from us always telling our kids exactly what to do. Communicating your wishes in an attuned way starts from the premise that you believe in your children's inner good and you will help them develop it.

Parents' Knee-Jerk Reactions

A mom shared a dinnertime blowup with us recently. At the table, both her son and her daughter wanted to be first to serve themselves the pasta, leading to a tug-of-war over the serving spoon. It all seemed ridiculous to the mom. "Stop it!" she commanded. "It doesn't matter who gets the food first!" The kids kept tugging and arguing. "Are you kidding me? I said stop it! This is crazy!" Her tone got louder and more frustrated. "Neither of you are getting the pasta and you're going straight to your rooms if you keep this up!" The kids kept yelling. The serving spoon went flying and smacked the ground and tomato sauce splattered everywhere. "Oh, perfect!" snapped the mom. She lamented that it was impossible for them to ever have a nice family meal.

This mom was understandably frustrated. Her words were ignored, the argument seemed silly, and her children knew better. So why didn't anyone listen to her? Why did a silly conflict escalate?

Jumping Into the Ring

As we talked, the mom uncovered the reason: when there's tension between her kids, her anxiety level rises quickly. In the case of the pasta dispute, when her kids started getting frustrated with each other, she was immediately irritated and focused on making the behavior stop, so she missed the chance to help them. With their building tension, they were telling her they could use understanding and help. In yelling at them, she missed this opening, and the conflict escalated. This is an *offensive*, versus *attuned*, move. Offensive moves escalate or intimidate.

What attuned move could the mom have made? She could have lowered her body to their level and described what she saw, as the sportscaster, asked a question to understand better, or helped the kids listen to each other. She could have started with, *Okay, wow. Big feelings about serving pasta. Fill me in.* If her kids didn't stop the spoon tug-of-war, then: *I'm taking the spoon for a moment because I can see this thing might go flying. Now talk to me—what's going on?* They might still be angry at each other, but her nonjudgmental questions would give them a chance to practice conflict resolution.

It's normal to get upset when kids aren't listening. The problem is that when you jump into the ring, your child's defenses go up and her brain goes into fight-or-flight mode. Either she'll become more adversarial or she'll squash her ideas because you've scared her. Meeting her with attunement is the way to engage cooperation. If you approach with a sense that you are trying to understand and be helpful (not just rush and order her around), her defenses are lowered. Now you can work together.

Inevitably, a parent in our groups will question us on this tactic. "But I'm the parent! I get to tell her what to do and I want to be listened to! If I'm understanding, she won't respect my authority. She already *knows* the right way to behave; I shouldn't have to talk about it." The first part is true: you are the parent and you are in charge.

The second part is not true. If your child feels understood by you (even when she's being difficult or misbehaving), she reaps enormous emotional and cognitive benefits, and the two of you stay connected. And even though kids technically "know" rules, there's a difference between knowing them and putting them into practice in the moment. You might "know" that your partner hates it when you interrupt, but you might still do it over and over before learning another way—and you're a grown-up! Kids need you to guide them in applying those rules and limits in everyday life.

Threatening and Bribing

Charles was at the park with his preschooler. A curious little explorer, she kept wandering around and experimenting with picking things up and getting involved in the games other kids were playing. She wandered to a pair of jump-roping big kids and started grabbing the rope, which interrupted the game. "Riley, no. Don't grab that," said her dad. She kept walking over and reaching for it. Her dad scooped her up and carried her away, and then sat back down on a bench. She waddled back. After repeating this a couple of times to no avail, Charles added a threat. "Riley, stop it. Wanna go to time-out?" Now Riley started to cry and eventually threw herself on the pavement. Her dad was stumped and wondered why even the smallest trip to the park seemed like so much work.

Was Riley misbehaving? No, she was showing her dad what developmental skills she was working on (including impulse control), by testing and experimenting with the different playthings at the park. She needed to be understood, shown what she *could* do, given alternatives, and she probably needed her dad to engage with her and play, rather than reacting after the fact.

We've all had those moments, when threatening or bribing seem like the only choices. Every parent knows how tempting this can be as a way of making kids do what we want them to do.

Okay, you're not putting your shoes on? Then I'm leaving without you.

I said play nicely. Do you want to go to time-out?

If you don't do your homework now, no more screen time tonight.

You want to stay home from the party tonight? Do you want me to leave you with Dad?

If you make a basket in the game tonight, I'll buy you a doughnut.

The urge to threaten with a consequence or bribe with a reward is so understandable. When we're ignored or disregarded, it can make us feel stuck, powerless, and angry. We lose patience and we run out of options—we want compliance and sometimes these feel like the only options that gives us leverage. We feel it too as moms ourselves. It can be maddening to not be listened to.

Threatening and bribing can work in the short term, but there are so many reasons not to do it. For one, it sends the message that you don't believe your child is willing and able to do the right thing without fearing a consequence or needing a reward. That's not the path you want to go down. Over time, it becomes less and less effective—all the while your child isn't developing her own initiative or ability to make good choices; she's just becoming more ashamed and resentful and more likely to hide her feelings from you. These tactics also send an inherently distasteful or negative message about the task you're trying to get done. *Straight to bed without stories* means that bed is a bad place to go. *No dessert unless you eat your vegetables* means vegetables aren't yummy. *If you make a basket you get a dough-nut* means performance is for the parent's sake, not the innate desire or drive. Day-to-day life can become burdensome and negative when we're constantly being lured and controlled into complying. On page 213 you'll see how to use natural consequences and logical information to engage cooperation instead.

Pleading, Negotiating, Caving

On the other hand, parents can tip too far toward the permissive side by overexplaining, endlessly negotiating, or caving on important limits. When this happens, kids feel anxious and confused, and often they cry harder, yell louder, or dig in their heels even more because they don't trust the limit. We see parents engage in endless pleading that ends in caving. Kids don't pick up their toys, clear their dishes, or set the table, so do it for them. They don't get dressed, so we chase them down and wrestle them into their clothes. They don't brush their teeth, so we let them skip it. Children learn that if they protest, they will not have to do whatever it is they are resisting. When you use ALP, do not overtalk, cajole, or endlessly debate your every move. Attunement can be conveyed by a quick phrase or even a look or your body language, before you state your limit and problem solve.

We're going to help you communicate your wishes and engage cooperation in both an attuned and effective way. It takes work, but even if you can manage it 25 percent of the time, you've made great strides. There will always be moments when the urge to yell, threaten, or cave is too strong and your patience is tapped out. That's okay. This is a practice—a way of being that we're reaching for as parents and will never do perfectly every time.

ALP FOR LISTENING AND COOPERATION

Prepare. Give your child a head's up.

Attune. Let your child know you understand. Join in or say what you see ("sportscasting").

You're really into your movie, I can see that.

Your toys are still on the floor.

I notice dishes on the table.

Limit set. State limits, family rules, and requests. Say what you *do* want.

It's time to turn it off now because we're getting ready to leave.

Put dishes on the kitchen counter, please.

Problem solve. Propose, "Here's what you *can* do." Use natural consequences.

Press pause and let's race to see who gets shoes on first.

Should we pretend we're waiters and it's time to clear the table for dessert?

Prepare

It helps to have a preparation step for times when you know that following a rule might be hard, or for transitions like coming to dinner, turning off screens, or leaving the house, a store, or a fun place. Say something like

> *You guys chose to sit together. I know you can make each other have lots of energy. Just checking this feels like it'll work for both of you.*

> *Just a heads-up, we're going to the bathtub in five minutes.*

> *It's almost time to turn off the video game. Do your last moves and get to a place you can shut it off.*

> *I know you guys are having fun! We're going to leave soon, so do your last thing.*

If your child can tell time, you can give him a specific agreed-on time. Say,

> *Check the clock with me. See how it's five minutes until our stopping time? Get to a place you can turn it off in five minutes.*

We sometimes hear parents overdo it with preparation, meaning that they yell out a "warning" for five minutes, but they do it for thirty minutes straight, every five or ten minutes yelling out an arbitrary time limit. Wait until you really know a transition is coming, and see if you can stick to the time frame. Use a neutral tone rather than a warning one.

You can also prepare by talking about expectations at the place you'll be. If the supermarket or a restaurant has been tricky for you, say in the car ride,

> *We're heading to the market. Can you guys remind me of what we do there? Things like, we can either walk next to the cart or sit in the front of the cart. Anything else?*

Attune

Attuning will involve making an empathic statement, narrating, or asking a question. Most people naturally start with the limit—*You can't do that. No. That's not okay*—so don't worry if you forget the attune step. It takes practice to add it in, and you can always circle back if you forget (even later that day!).

As you read this section, circle the phrases that sound right to you, or write versions for yourself based on these ideas. All of the tools in this section are helpful, but you won't use every one of them every time.

Let's say you've asked your child to come to the table for dinner and he doesn't do it. Rather than getting louder and more insistent, give him the benefit of the doubt. He's engrossed in a game, has a desire of his own in that moment, is overstimulated, or wants your attention. Kids don't ignore directions because they're trying to be difficult. They have their own needs, agendas, and mental worlds. The best place to start when you're engaging cooperation is to make a connection to that inner world.

Attune Tool #1:
Join

Check in and see what your child is up to. Before repeating your request or stating a limit again, make an observation or joining statement like

Cool. I see you're working hard on that puzzle.

Ah, I get now why you don't want to come to the table yet. That tower is getting super tall.

I know, it's not easy to pause this game when you're right in the middle of it.

I still see pj's on you! You're having a hard time getting ready for school.

Connect before you make your request again. Just the act of being seen makes kids more likely to cooperate. Simply walking over and getting on her level, and maybe touching your child on the shoulder, even without words, makes her feel like she's not being shuttled and commanded. When you do this, you lower your child's defenses. Now she's more receptive to what you have to say. How would you want your loved one to call you for dinner if you were curled up on the couch reading a cliff-hanger or halfway through writing a time-sensitive e-mail?

Julie helped her son this way one morning when he was having a hard time getting out of bed. Instead of nudging and taking off his covers or telling him he'd be late, she sat on the side of the bed and said, *You're all cozy under your covers. It's hard to get out of bed on a cold morning and get ready for school, isn't it?* She paused. He rolled toward her and looked at her like she was from Mars. He clearly felt understood. It took him just another minute to uncover himself and climb out.

Attune Tool #2:
Say What You See: The Sportscaster

Describe what's happening in front of you, like a sportscaster doing a play-by-play in a factual, nonjudgmental way.

I notice your shoes are not on your feet.

The dishes are still on the table.

I'm giving you information right now, but you're not looking at me. It's hard to tell if you hear me or not.

Avoid asking "I think you did something wrong here" questions, like

What's your problem, why don't you ever listen to me?

What did you do now?

How many times do I have to tell you?

Attune Tool #3:
Use Your Iceberg Analogy

Think to yourself: *What's he trying to say? What's he working on? Why is he not listening?* If your son's being mean to his sister, is he angry at her or someone else? If your daughter's demanding you take off her shoes for her, is she wanting to connect with you after a long day of school? If your son is running in a restaurant, is he too tired or hungry to regulate himself? It doesn't mean that you should let meanness go, take your kid's shoes off for her every day, or allow crazy restaurant behavior. It just means you have the insight to see what's really going on. This is how you help your child articulate his or her desires and feelings in an appropriate way. If you skip straight to threatening and controlling, you miss that opportunity.

You know how to take off your own shoes (tip-of-the-iceberg statement).

Long day at school, huh. I've missed you. Lemme squeeze these feet for a sec (beneath-the-surface statement).

Be quiet! This behavior is unacceptable. Do you want to go to time-out? (tip-of-the-iceberg statement)

I see you're excited and moving all around! (Crouching down face-to-face, gently holding if needed.) *I know, this restaurant is loud and you're hungry. Let's take a breather outside* (beneath-the-surface statement).

When you stop to consider *why* your child is acting the way she is, it can feel like a pressure release, like air going out of a balloon. It's not personal, and it's not meant to push your buttons.

FROM HEATHER

One morning, I heard my four-year-old grumbling about not being able to find a Lego cat she wanted to play with. She started riffling through the bin in frustration and, next thing I knew, a Lego carriage went flying through the air. The tip of the iceberg would tell me to say, "Hey, no throwing toys!" Or even just "What are you doing?" in a tsk-tsk voice. I knew what was going on under the surface, though, so I went over, sat on the rug, and put a hand on her shoulder. "Wow, frustrated, huh? I heard you say you couldn't find the cat?" She sighed and nodded. I could tell her guard came down a little. She didn't really *want* to throw a toy, but her four-year-old frustration tolerance was low in that moment. We looked for the cat together.

Limit Set

Here you will state a rule, or family agreement (page 194), give information, or make a request, along with an explanation if applicable. For example,

> *It's too much splashing for this pool because there are smaller kids.*

> *Okay, it's time to leave the house. Let's put our shoes on.*

> *We have to go inside, because it's raining. Please walk with me.*

> *I'm not okay with you talking to me that way.*

Adding to the previous attuned statements, it would sound something like this,

> *Cool. I see you're working hard on that puzzle. It's bath time now.*

> *Ah, I get now why you don't want to come to the table yet. That tower is getting super tall. Now the food's ready, so it's time to sit down for dinner.*

> *I know, it's hard to pause this game when you're right in the middle of it. I need help cleaning the living room, so let's all work on that together now.*

> *I still see pj's on you! You're having a hard time getting ready for school. To get there before the bell rings, we have to leave in three minutes.*

FAMILY AGREEMENTS

Family agreements are unique to your family, although there will be overlap with those of other families too. It's nice for kids to feel as though their family has certain ways of operating and understandings among each other that are special. Family agreements are expectations of all the members. You may want to write them down, especially if there's a repeated issue with one of them. These are just examples. Create your own and be ready to change them as time goes on. On our website (nowsaythisbook.com) you'll see a tool for creating your own family agreements.

ROSEN FAMILY AGREEMENTS

We are safe with each other's bodies.

We speak kindly to each other and don't name-call.

At the dinner table we eat and talk. Toys and devices are parked.

We ask to be excused before we get up.

Everyone helps get dinner on the table and clean up after.

We help each other.

When someone spills something, we all do our best to help clean it up.

When one person is hurt (even if it's not our fault), we check in.

Use your family meetings (page 59) to review or amend family agreements if needed. Agreements serve the same purpose as "rules," but they give a sense of collaboration and partnership. Framing them as what you've agreed to do, rather than a list of don't-do's, is much more helpful and positive.

Limit-Setting Tool #1:
Say What You DO Want and What Your Child CAN Do

Tell your kids what they CAN do. This is a simple and useful way of talking for the whole family (coach siblings to use it with each other). It's easier for kids to follow directions when they have something *to do*, rather than simply being asked *not to* or to cut off an impulse.

(Instead of) *Stop running in the store!*

(Say) *Please hold my hand through the store.*

(Instead of) *Get your toys off the table!*

(Say) *Oh, wait, remember at the table we only eat and talk. Let's park our toys in the living room.*

(Instead of) *Shhh! Stop yelling!*

(Say) *Use an inside voice in here. It's important because other people are trying to talk and eat.*

(Instead of) *No pushing! Say you're sorry!*

(Say) *Looks like you were trying to say, "I need space." Can you give her those words?*

Limit-Setting Tool #2:
Kneel Down and Give Clear Information

Instead of shouting from across the house or repeating yourself ten times, if you aren't listened to, go to your child, get down on her level or below, and talk clearly and calmly. If it's not an immediate rush, pause and convey that you're not impatiently demanding her compliance, you're genuinely checking in, while making a request or stating a family rule.

A dad told us that this was easy to do for simple requests, but when his kids were misbehaving and breaking rules, he got angry quickly and went straight to raising his voice and threatening again. One day his sons were splashing and jumping in the pool in a way that was too rowdy. It irritated him because he'd told them so many times before about this. After he shouted their names a few times and they ignored him, he could feel himself wanting to scream angrily, "Stop splashing or we're going home!" But instead, he started by walking over to them while thinking for a second. First of all, the threat he had in his head wasn't a good one, because he was enjoying his time at the pool and didn't *want* to leave. He considered, *What exactly do I want them to do? What information do they need?* He went to the side of the pool, knelt down, and said in a loud enough voice, "Boys! Quick second over here." And motioned for them to join him. "You're splashing and having such a good time, I can see that. There are little kids in the pool, so watch around you. When you're the biggest ones, look out for taking care of the little ones."

NOT SURE WHAT TO SAY?
BUY YOURSELF SOME TIME.

You don't always have to have the right answer on the spot. And sometimes when you give an impulsive answer, you regret it later because you say something you can't or don't want to follow through on. It's good to make our process transparent for kids. Buy yourself some time by saying,

> *You know what, I'm not sure. I need a few minutes to think about this.*

> *I'm figuring out what to do here, so let me get back to you on that.*

> *I hear your point. Let me think about that.*

This also allows you to be more flexible in how you respond. You can mindfully assess the situation and think about what's best in that particular moment. There is not a one-size-fits-all set of rules or best way to handle every situation.

Limit-Setting Tool #3:
Inform and Entice in Place of Bribes

You can entice or motivate without bribing. You do this by giving the information in a way that lets kids know something will happen after they've achieved the task. It's a slight change of words and tone, but it's meaningful. Instead of *If you do your homework you can have some*

TV time, or, *If you clean your room we can go to the park,* with an over-selling, cajoling tone, try an informational tone:

> *When you've finished your homework, we'll watch TV.*

> *When we've put the toys away, we'll go to the park.*

> *When you've picked out your clothes for tomorrow, let's snuggle up and start reading books.*

> *When you turn off your iPad, we'll work on that puzzle together.*

> *Let's get our shoes on and get into the car. Who's picking the music?*

This conveys that you believe your children are capable and will cooperate. The more you interact with this premise, the more they will grow into this ability.

A super-skilled preschool teacher we know tells us that, after rest time, when the children are supposed to be putting their cots away and cleaning up, if there's a lot of dillydallying, the teacher gives information to naturally entice by saying something like

> *Sometimes taking a long time makes it hard to get to the yard for outside time. I don't want you to miss your favorite game in the grass!*

Limit-Setting Tool #4:
Use Humor

One mom told us that if she said her son's name a few times and he didn't respond, she'd sing it instead. Dig deep to find humor or playfulness—this will shift the dynamic and make you both more flexible. Wordlessly put a pair of pants on your head and when your daughter points and laughs, say, *Oh, jeez, why are these on my head and not your legs?* Or, *I'm sorry, but did someone hit the "off" button on Hannah? Because she's not getting dressed or moving on her steps for getting out the door. Now, if I just had the instruction manual I could— ooh, got it.*

If you yell in an attempt to get something done, it can backfire. Your child may dig in her heels, or she may comply out of fear or a desire to calm you down.

WHINING, COMPLAINING, AND NAGGING

Say What You DO Want. Use Your Normal Words.

Whining is a sign that your child is frustrated and needs your help. It's so hard to listen to whining and so tempting to just want it to stop. Try, though, to understand why she's frustrated and help her communicate this in a better way.

You can use a simple statement in response to whining that comes in very handy:

> *I can tell you're having a hard time. When you say that in a normal or regular voice, I'll be ready to listen.*

> *You sound frustrated. Can you use your regular voice so I can help you better?*

Say this without raising your voice or snapping, but rather in a nonchalant, "I'll wait for as long as I need to, no hurries" kind of way. If your child needs a hug, be ready to give one. You can still make your request for a normal voice. Rather than saying, "Use your big-girl voice" (which is fine, but a little condescending), just let your child know you're ready to help when she asks with regular words.

In Heather's family, when someone frames their statements in a negative way, they use the phrase, *Say what you want, not what you don't want.* It helps turn whining and complaining into requests that are better articulated and understood. When you hear a negative whine, say

> *I'm hearing a lot of what you don't like, not what you'd like to happen. What's your idea?*

> *Can you tell me what you want, not what you don't want? That way I can help you.*

> *Tell me what you'd like to happen, not what you don't want to happen.*

A lovely mom of three found it virtually impossible to keep from snapping at her youngest daughter, who was following her around nagging and interrupting her while Mom was busy. "Mama, Mama, Mama," she would say in the middle of the mom's conversations, and then she'd unleash a complaint. Mom tried to catch this early, before it snowballed. She got on her daughter's level and said,

> *You need something from me, I can tell, but I am not okay with you talking to me this way.* (She thought for a second about how tired her daughter was and how she wanted Mom's attention.) She said, *I know, there are a lot of people around so my focus is split. I wish I could give you all of my attention right now. When everyone leaves, we'll snuggle and read together, just us.*

Limit-Setting Tool #5:
Know When to Be Flexible

When you set limits mindfully, you consider your child in that particular moment, rather than sticking to rules just for the sake of sticking to them. We're not suggesting to go back on important limits (like those involving safety or kindness), but, of course, there are moments for exceptions to rules and flexibility.

Consider whether something is a "gotta-do" and nonnegotiable, like brushing teeth, putting on the right shoes for school, sitting down in a restaurant, coming to the table for dinner, or having good social etiquette, or a "let's talk about it" moment, like stopping at the park on the way home, spending more time at a friend's house even though you said it was time to go, or staying up late to finish a movie. If kids have the sense that their "gotta-dos" are solid and trusted, they end up being able to roll with the "let's talk about it" moments more easily. A colleague of ours says to her kids, *Sometimes it's my decision, sometimes it's your decision, and sometimes we decide together.*

What about when you change your mind? Although constant flip-flopping can create anxiety and confusion, it's also not bad to change course. In families that listen to each other's wishes and feelings, there is always discussion—that's good.

> *I thought about it a little more, listened to what you said and talked to Dad as well, and decided you can go to the sleepover. Let's talk about it beforehand and go over some information.*

> *I realize I made a mistake when I said you could play with the iPad today. It's not a good choice because you have other projects and we need to make space in the day for those.*

Limit-Setting Tool #6:
With a Strong-Willed Child, Use a Firm, Confident Voice

If you have a strong-willed, persistent child, then you already know you put more energy into holding clear and consistent limits. Kids with these personality traits need us to communicate rules and limits in a firm voice, and sometimes while moving or holding their bodies (for example, if they're going to hurt someone else). You can attune while also clearly letting your child know *I will stop you. I will hold this limit for you as many times as you need me to before you learn it.* Using a firm voice does not mean yelling, it means sending the message to your child that, no matter what, you are unwavering and you will enforce this rule or limit to help him every single time.

Limit-Setting Tool #7:
Spread the "Help Each Other" Mentality

I didn't drop it. I didn't do it! It's not my stuff, I don't have to pick it up. Sometimes it can feel like it's every person for him- or herself. Model a "help each other" mentality with your children and eventually it will become a family value that everyone in the household is familiar with. When you need help, ask your children to help you:

I need help getting dinner going; could someone run the Brussels sprouts under water at the sink?

Everything fell out of my bag. S.O.S., I need my picker-uppers!

And when they need help, you help them:

Oh, wow, you have a lot of paper scraps here on the floor, let me help you.

Oops, your glass tipped over. I'll toss you a sponge.

Engender in your children not just a willingness but a desire to help others. We're all part of the family and we're all happy to help each other. Everyday life is full of so many mundane, repetitive tasks. If we make our kids feel burdened by that, it's not so fun.

CHORES AND RESPONSIBILITIES

A client told us about having dinner at a friend's home. They had a family with kids visiting from Denmark. After dinner, the Danish kids jumped up and started clearing the table, putting things away, and even loading the dishwasher. As if it was the most normal thing in the world. Our client was dumbfounded and impressed. "Why didn't I teach my kids to do this? I forgot an entire part of parenting!"

Kids like to be needed. It's a good feeling to be seen as a capable, contributing member from an early age. Having kids help out often falls by the wayside because it's easier and faster to pick up their clothes, prepare the dinner, and clean up the house on our own than to teach and monitor them. For many families, attempts at instilling chores or daily tasks backfire and end up in power struggles and frustration.

You can turn chores and tasks into opportunities to feel good about contributing. Discuss this at family and couples meetings (pages 59 and 61) so you can come up with a thoughtful plan rather than having those nagging, helpless feelings that your kids should help out more.

Mommy, Daddy, What Can I Do to Help?

Get in the habit of having your kids ask you every day, "What can I do to help?" (One partner can discreetly prompt the child to say this to the other partner.) You ask too—it's a two-way street. You're setting a tone of caring and being attuned to each other's needs. It's the opposite of being self-centered. We don't intend to raise self-centered kids, but if we only focus on their schoolwork, their activities, and their needs, we are doing so unwittingly. It takes a clear intention to add in a focus on "other" to counter all the "me, me" focus inherent in their world.

Assume Your Child (Even Your Toddler)
Is Capable

Little kids love to help. The problem is that, because they're messy and uncoordinated, we often don't include them, so we miss out on the chance to support and cultivate this love when it's strong. You won't always be able to include your toddler, but look for opportunities. She can wash the string beans, sort the socks, put napkins and plastic dishes on the table, and so forth. Even if she *feels* like she's helping, it counts. You can get (or make) a child's step stool with safety railings and let your little one rinse vegetables in the sink, stir something, or transfer berries from one bowl to another. She can help you hold your list or an item from it in the store.

In our toddler classes, we've learned that even the youngest ones, at thirteen or fourteen months, begin to help with cleanup if we do it a certain way. The key is using an opaque laundry bag (a clear bin makes grabbing the toys back out too tempting) and having the parents start to put the toys into the bag very slowly, one by one. If we do those two simple things, before long, the toddlers start picking up toys and putting them in the bag. It's fascinating. The hardest part is preventing the parents from scooping up all the toys quickly. It's exactly the same at home. If you can slow down, be patient, and give kids time to imitate you, they will show you what they can do.

Keep the Bar High—You'll Be Surprised

We often meet parents who are still doing all kinds of things for their children that the children are very capable of doing themselves, such as helping them all the way to sleep, spoon-feeding them, or getting them all the way dressed. What's the downside to this? It does not foster independence, and eventually it can lead to resentment on their part, and yours too. It feels good to kids when they have responsibility for tasks they're capable of doing.

Once when Julie's son was nine years old, a friend of hers came over for dinner. When the friend walked into the kitchen, Jack was happily slicing veggies and salmon with a large knife, in preparation for the stir-fry he was making. The friend was terrified, certain he must be breaking a rule. He couldn't possibly be capable or safe. But he was! He had been cooking from an early age and loved planning and preparing his masterpieces. He had learned how to handle a knife safely. This is an example of where years of patience with spills, undeveloped skills, and mistakes paid off in the long run. Now he's a college student who cooks most of his own food and saves a ton of money.

Set Up the Environment for Success

Adjust your child's environment so he can do more on his own when he's quite young. Place pegs where he can reach to hang his jacket, pj's, towels, and so forth. Relegate a drawer or shelf in the kitchen and fridge with cups, bowls, plates, utensils, drinks, and snacks in a place he can reach. Do the same for clothing, toys, books, and anything else you can think of that will help him be more independent. Preschools provide great examples of these ideas. It's always amazing to parents to see their kids pouring from little pitchers around the lunch table. You can do the same at home. Start with a little bit of water and watch them master this skill. A colleague showed us a video of her daughter at her preschool at the Mother's Day lunch. She very carefully poured her mom about a tablespoon of orange juice into a cup. She couldn't have been more proud of herself!

Do It Together

Little kids love to imitate their parents and older siblings. Use this love to bring them alongside you. Invite him to help you carry the trash out, load and unload the dishwasher, put the clothes in the washer or dryer, or sweep the floor (what toddler doesn't love to hold a broom?).

Our culture tends to value independence and personal responsibility, but if you really think about what makes us all feel like part of a family or community, it's helping each other and doing things together. It's so much more fun that way and we can chat and joke as we work. The job gets done quickly and might not even feel like work. In Heather's house, they call it "hoteling," as in making their home look as neat and clean as a hotel room. They put on music and everyone participates until every room is hoteled. One dad we know says to his kids, "Okay, we're all gonna find ten things to pick up or put away, and meet back in the kitchen when we're done." It's like a race and his kids run around looking for things that are out of place. This also develops the valuable skill of "reading a room." How many times have you marveled that someone leaves their dishes or clothes out without a clue that they're even there? It's not only about learning how to clean up but the consideration of others that's involved. Use language that portrays the family as a team, whose members each need to do their jobs to solve problems and accomplish goals. For example,

> *Okay, let's see, we have to leave the house for Sammy's soccer game. We're a team, so what do we need to do to get it all together? I'm going to pack my bag. Sammy, you're in charge of getting your cleats and water bottle . . .*

Avoid Scolding with Mistakes and Spills

When someone spills or drops something, it's a sweet opportunity to rush over and help them. Whether they're capable of cleaning it on their own, this is still a kind response. When our kids spill or break something unintentionally, not only do they not need to be reprimanded or scolded, they need to be empathized with and helped. They already feel bad enough and they need us to understand that. When they're grown up and their good friend or loved one has some kind of mishap, how do we hope they will react? These moments are all opportunities to learn and practice a caring way of being.

Stay Positive

Resist the urge to correct or criticize when kids are helping. When they're really tiny, their help is largely symbolic. Your daughter may be digging in the garden "helping" you plant some new flowers or your son may be wielding his toy broom, kicking up dust and having a grand time as he is "helping" you sweep. You can always go back later and get things the way you want them, when your child isn't there. You can gently show him and teach him, but be careful not to constantly find fault.

Replace Nagging with Visual Charts

Visual charts with pictures and/or words can be extremely helpful. Transferring your family rules about chores and tasks from verbal reminders into a colorful chart can change the dynamic from resistance to "I know what to do—I just look at my chart!" It's such a relief to not have to nag. You can decide what kinds of charts best suit your family's needs. We work with many families to design before- and after-school charts, Saturday chore charts, and bedtime routine charts. Have your kids help create them and adjust them as they grow. Then you can just nod or point to their chart instead of asking them for the seventh time to brush their teeth or get their clothes on. These charts and lists can be reviewed and discussed at family meetings. See tools on our website (nowsaythisbook.com) for creating visual charts.

Problem Solve

Problem solving when kids aren't listening is a tricky one, and it takes a big dose of patience and humor.

Remember that your little one's brain is steadily working on self-regulation, self-discipline, and creativity. This is an opening for her to flex these mental muscles. Don't worry if it doesn't "work" at first. Depending on her age and personality, she may need to hear you talk this way many times before she's able to offer her input. She really needs to get the sense that there's not always one right way, and that there is space for her ideas.

Problem-Solving Tool #1:
Propose "Here's What You Can Do"

Offer an alternative way to fulfill your child's intention.

Cool. I see you're working hard on that puzzle. It's bath time now. Let's put your puzzle in a safe place so you can keep working on it tomorrow.

Ah, I get now why you haven't come to the table yet. That tower is getting super tall. Now the food's ready, so it's time to sit down to dinner. Let's put a "work in progress" sticky note on that tower.

I get it, it's hard to pause this game when you're right in the middle of it. I need help cleaning the living room, so let's all work on that together now. You do have ten minutes of game time left today, so you could do that after we clean up.

I still see pj's on you! You're having a hard time getting ready for school. To get there before the bell rings, we have to leave in three minutes. I'm going to put two outfits out, side by side. Don't look until they're ready . . . Okay, go choose.

In some cases, you may have to offer a follow-through choice (page 136).

Problem-Solving Tool #2:
Use the "Bumbling Parent"

If your child is upset, it doesn't mean you have to be too—take a deep breath and let her feelings flow under your boat. Let them be okay. This will help you stay open and solve problems. Instead of raising your voice or rushing to fix things, switch the dynamic and use a "hmm, I don't know, what do you think we could do here?" tone. Kids often find the head-scratching, bumbling parent pretty interesting, which is always helpful with getting them involved in problem solving. This does not mean you're going back on your limit, if it's a "gotta-do," nonnegotiable one. If the limit is that your toddler needs to hold your hand crossing the street, you might say, *We always hold hands to cross the street to stay safe, so hmm, let's see, what could we do . . .* (Pause so she has the chance to interject something. If she doesn't have an idea, offer one.) *We could both be in charge of looking left and right when we cross.*

FROM HEATHER: GETTING OUT OF THE HOUSE

One morning, time was ticking and my daughter needed to get her shoes on, but she was starting to play with a doll. I knew I only had about five more minutes to leave before we'd be late. I went over to where she was playing, near the couch, and squatted down and watched for a second before saying,

"I see you're starting to play with that doll, but it's time to put shoes on."

"I have to put the pants on the doll first."

"Hmm, what do you think . . . ?" (Pausing to "scratch my head" as if to genuinely wonder.) "Do you think we have enough time for that before we go, or does it seem like it's too big of a job for right now?"

"I can do it, it's just a little more . . ." (Struggles with the pants a bit.) "No, it's too much. I'll have to take it with me in the car."

By being the bumbling parent and giving her a chance to choose the solution, she didn't get the feeling from me that I'd be plucking her out of what she was into. She was able to be receptive to problem solving.

Problem-Solving Tool #3:
Find Common Ground

Instead of butting heads and arguing, listen to what your child is telling you he wants. Look for opportunities to take his ideas and desires into account. Don't be afraid to negotiate and find common ground.

A parent told us that, with her strong-willed child, she had to look for opportunities to say yes, rather than being rigid about all of her limits and directions. One day her daughter said she wanted to meet a friend at the park. "Not today. Too much to do," said the mom. "Please, Mom! Please, please, I really want to go. I haven't seen her all week!" Mom paused and thought about it. "I can see you really want to go. Talk to me about it and tell me your idea. Dinnertime is soon, and we still haven't done homework or had a bath, so how would it work?" For this mom, doing homework and eating a good dinner were must-dos. Her daughter shared a few ideas and the two came to common ground: First finish homework, while the mom called the parent of the friend, and they all pitched in to make a picnic and bring it to the park for dinner. The daughter agreed to have a shower the next morning instead of a bath.

Problem Solving Tool #4:
Use Natural Consequences in Place of Punishments

When we feel stuck and frustrated, sometimes we try arbitrary consequences or punishments like *You said something mean to your sister, so no screens for the rest of the day.* Or, *If you don't stay in bed all night, you won't go to the party tomorrow.* These punishments do very little to teach, and they definitely do not help build trust and connection.

However, the world will deliver its own natural consequences—don't be afraid to let these happen. When consequences are logical and make sense for the situation, they're helpful learning tools and we should not shield our kids from experiencing them. For example,

> *It seems like it's hard to stop bouncing this ball in the house. I'm going to put it away until we go to the park.*

> *You're showing me that you can't be in the bath together right now. I'm going to lift one of you out.*

> *Seems like using the iPad before practice isn't working; we can both see how it's getting really hard to turn it off. I'm going to take it for now since you're having a hard time sticking to our plan.*

> *I know, you wish the T-shirt was clean so you could wear it. But Daddy and I only wash the clothes that are in the hamper.*

> *Ah, I see the teacher marked your homework as incomplete, because you didn't do it last night.*

It can be hard to let go and allow for natural consequences when it comes to school and other aspects of life that we, as parents, care so much about. But when we do this, it helps our kids develop what is called an "internal locus of control"—the sense of optimism that comes from knowing you can affect your environment and that you have control over your life. This feeling of control is highly linked to greater well-being, lower rates of anxiety and depression, and more. Allowing your fourth grader to do poorly on a test because he chose not to study (you reminded him and offered to quiz him, but he said no) gives him the chance to feel the natural consequences, and on the flip side, feel the sense of agency when he does study. Parents sometimes mask this process when they overhelp or make unilateral decisions. Use the concept of scaffolding (page 240). As your child gets older and more capable, you help less and less, while he takes over more decisions—even when it means not getting a good grade. This will make him more likely to become internally motivated in the future.

You can plant these seeds when kids are little. A couple we worked with, Mark and Tina, had two daughters, one in preschool and one in second grade. Morning was a nightmare. No one got dressed, brushed teeth, or put shoes on without the parents nagging and getting incredibly frustrated. They struggled to get their girls out of the house on time on school and work days. The second-grader, although totally capable of dressing herself and packing her backpack, would not take responsibility for these steps. The parents knew that yelling, threatening, and bribing wasn't ideal, but inevitably, they found themselves doing it anyway. They felt ineffective and came to dread the mornings.

When we met with them, we explored the idea of natural consequences. The parents agreed that their second-grader did not want to be late for school. She would be marked as tardy and have to bring a note with her explaining the reason. But the parents had never, not once, allowed this to happen. It seemed like the perfect natural consequence. They were pretty resistant to letting this happen—which speaks to our very understandable desire to protect our kids from making mistakes and being accountable for their actions. Finally they gave it a try. Sure enough, after just one time being late and dealing with the school's consequences, the daughter started taking much more responsibility for getting ready on time. Her newfound initiative rubbed off on her younger sister, who of course loved to imitate her.

Problem-Solving Tool #5:
Use a Follow-Through Choice

Sometimes despite our best efforts, we still feel stuck. Our kids won't listen or comply with our directions and limits, and maybe there's no obvious natural consequence. Remember it's a child's job to experiment and test the world, and sometimes it takes a hundred times of stating a limit and following through on it for the experiment to be over. Try not to get too frustrated with a toddler who repeatedly won't hold your hand, or a school-age child who balks at turning off a device even though you've told him twenty times in a row. When that happens, one of your choices in the problem-solving step can be a follow-through choice. This choice involves you physically stepping in to enforce the limit. Over time kids learn that they can't stall forever and the family will keep moving one way or another.

Try to be lighthearted and matter-of-fact about it. It's not a punishment, it's just a reality. It's important that you are always very gentle and calm. If you're angry and exasperated, take time to calm down first.

We hold hands to cross the street so we're safe. You can hold my hand or I can pick you up until we get across.

We're getting in the car because it's time to go. Do you want to walk on your own or should I help you into the car?

It's not a buying day. You can put the toy back on the shelf or I can do it for you.

It's time to turn screens off. You can pause the show or I can do it for you.

If you need to hold, move, or remove your child, let her know. This is a respectful way to communicate and shows that you won't just pluck her up without advising her. For example,

It seems like you're not listening to my words, so I'm going to move you somewhere where we can hear each other better.

I'm going to pick you up and move you out to the car, because we do have to go.

Problem-Solving Tool #6:
Use Calm Down instead of Time-Out

"Do you want to go to time-out?" is one of the most common phrases parents use when they want to be heard. Time-outs can make kids feel angry or bad about themselves, or scare them into complying, but this is not our goal. Moments when our kids ignore us, or do something they're not supposed to, show us they need our help building a skill and practicing the right thing to do, or that they're trying to tell us something. The last thing they need is to be isolated and punished. Nipping it in the bud with a time-out cuts off all that learning. Kids who fear time-out might curb their behaviors while you're watching, but they don't necessarily get any practice doing the right thing or communicating appropriately when the threat isn't there.

Use calm down (page 49) or gently remove your child if it's a logical moment to do so. For example,

Your toddler is yelling and running around a restaurant.

(Instead of) *You're going to time-out in the car!*

(Say) *I'm moving you outside the restaurant so we can find a calm space.*

Your child is whining, yelling, or crying at the dinner table.

(Instead of) *Stop it right now or you're going to time-out!*

(Say) *I'm going to move you away from the table so we can have calm-down space and figure this out.*

Your eight-year-old is at a birthday party and is starting to get overexcited, a little out of control, and disruptive.

(Instead of) *Hey, what are you doing? You need to listen to me or you're leaving. You're acting crazy!*

(Say) *Hey, honey, come with me into the other room for a sec. I gotta tell you something.*

Frame this in a helpful, not punitive way. It builds your kid's trust that you will always do your best to find a private place to help when he needs you, rather than embarrassing or reprimanding him in front of others.

⌇ BRUSHING TEETH ⌇

If brushing teeth has become a dreaded, twice-daily battle in your home, you're not alone. It's a common struggle. It makes sense when you think about it: you're standing over a small person, trying to get a stick with bristles into his mouth, when he'd rather be doing a hundred other things at that moment. Some parents cave and let it go; others resort to pleading, threatening, and eventually forcing the matter and then feeling terrible afterward. We get it—this is a tricky one.

Since most dentists would say that kids need a parent's help with brushing until about age eight, working out a good teeth-brushing system early can make a big difference.

Start by giving it a nonnegotiable, "gotta do it, we'll figure it out together" feeling. You can even act the head-scratching, bumbling parent: "Hmm, well, we gotta do it, so what could our plan be?" Don't let your child dream that there's a chance they can wriggle out of it. They will rely on that opening in the future.

After you've attuned and set a limit about brushing (*You don't feel like pausing your game to brush teeth, I know. We do brush twice a day to keep our teeth healthy. Remember how the dentist told us this is how we won't get a cavity?*), here are a few tips for the problem-solving step that we've created and learned from our client parents over the years.

Face the Mirror

Sit your small child up on the bathroom counter so that you're both facing the mirror. For this one, you have to be very careful to keep children safe by holding one arm around their waist. Have toothbrushes for both of you ready and loaded with toothpaste. Watch yourselves in the mirror. For some kids this is a game changer. You can try different things—*my turn on my teeth, your turn on your teeth, your turn on my teeth, and then my turn on your teeth,* for example (sounds crazy, but it really works to let them have a turn on your teeth).

For some kids, just slowing down and taking turns is all they need to be okay with teeth brushing. Get down on their level or bring them up to yours.

Brush Teeth before Stories and Songs

Make sure the fun, cuddly stuff comes after brushing teeth. If your kids know your turn is going to take twenty-five seconds of you counting in a funny voice or singing the alphabet, followed by their favorite books and a few bedtime songs, it will be much easier for them to get through it. Resist saying, "If you don't brush your teeth, we won't have time for books," and try the subtly different, "When your teeth are all brushed, we'll be ready for stories."

Play or Sing a Song

This one has lots of possibilities. You can play a song that you both like, a song that signals how long to brush, or one song for their turn and one for yours. Try singing to a familiar melody and making up a song about your day—like this one we freestyled in twenty seconds!

Today, today, we went to the park,
Played on the slide 'til it got dark,
Then we held hands and walked to the car,
Good thing is, it wasn't very far.

Get an Electric Toothbrush

Dentists we've spoken to recommend investing in a good quality electric toothbrush, because the cheaper ones do not have the same bristle technology and don't clean anywhere near so effectively. Over time, they're also the more affordable option, because they last longer. Electric toothbrushes can make brushing way more fun.

Start from the First Tooth

This may surprise you, but the time to start brushing is when your baby's first teeth start coming in (the average age is about five months). This is what dentists recommend, as brushing of baby teeth is critical to the health of their adult teeth. At this age, babies are also much more open to it and you can easily make it fun and get a little swipe of those teeth in. It can be quick, but make it part of your routine twice a day, something that you always do, like eating breakfast or taking baths. This will make it much easier when they are toddlers.

Don't Force It

There will be times when nothing works. Resist the very normal urge to force it. Ask your child to give you three seconds and that's all. Tell them to open wide, count to three really slowly, and it will be done.

From Julie: Puppets as Helpers

When my son was little, we had a monkey puppet, named Fuzzy, and he was helpful for tricky moments like brushing teeth. He was very empathic: "Hey, I don't like this teeth-brushing stuff either." He knew the rules: "I know, I know, it's a 'gotta-do.'" And he was so great at comical problem solving: "Hey, you can brush mine first and then I'll brush yours, okay? Gotta get all this banana outta my teeth!" Just the addition of "Fuzzy's turn" was often enough to help my son accept his own turn. Puppets are great at defusing power struggles and they can often align with how your child feels while also modeling making good choices. Your kids don't feel so alone and they also feel like the puppet is showing them that they too will survive the dreaded brushing of the teeth.

From Heather

When my daughter isn't moving to the bathroom to brush her teeth, I call out, to no one in particular, "Oh, man, here I am in my dentist office, hoping to clean teeth, but no one is showing up. It's lonely in here. Now if only a patient would join . . . Oh my gosh, someone's here!" She thinks it's hilarious for me to pretend to be her dentist and have her surprise me for an appointment.

Problem-Solving Tool #7:
Brainstorm Separate from the Moment

If there's a part of the day that is repeatedly a problem, address it outside of that moment. At a time when you're not upset, say something like

> *I've noticed when I ask you to clean your room, you say no and it gets really tricky. What could we do?*

> *Okay, so we've agreed that I'm going to give you a three-minute heads-up before it's time to clean your room. Then you are going to choose some good cleanup music and I'll come in every five minutes to admire your progress. That right? Okay, let's see how it goes.*

Listen to your child's ideas (however random), write some down together, or brainstorm the ones that help you accomplish your goals and also make your child feel heard. Bring these recurring stuck points up at your family meeting.

Problem-Solving Tool #8:
Narrate instead of Saying "Good Job!"

It's tempting to praise when kids help, listen, and do what you're hoping they'll do. The downside of broad sweeping statements of praise is that they can sound empty and general, and it makes kids less likely to try again next time. Praise can also be somewhat like backhanded compliments if they come out sounding as if your child is normally difficult or incapable, but has *finally* done what she should. You don't want your child hung up on your evaluation—you want to direct her attention to *her* feelings about her accomplishments.

Instead of

Good job, you cleaned your room finally!

Wow, you brushed your teeth. You get a sticker!

Yay, you made me proud. Good job!

Say,

You folded your laundry and put away toys. It's such a pleasure to walk into your room. How does it feel to you?

Let's see how sparkly those teeth are!

I saw you working hard on that. How does it feel to be done?

Wow, I saw that!

You did it!

Look at you!

The best "praise" is descriptive. So if you're wondering what to say, look at what your child is doing, pick an aspect or detail, and describe. You don't have to overthink this or worry too much if you naturally gush with positivity. Just try to connect with what your child is feeling and working on, rather than it always being about your evaluation.

Scripts and Conversations

Scripts

Baby

SCENARIO: *Your baby stands in the bathtub and doesn't want to sit down. He repeatedly pops up to stand in the water.*

ATTUNE	LIMIT SET	PROBLEM SOLVE
You like standing in the tub, huh?	In the tub we sit down, because you could fall and hurt yourself.	You're showing me it's too hard to stay sitting down right now, so I'm going to wash you quickly and lift you out of the tub. We'll try playing in the bath tomorrow.

SCENARIO: *Your baby crawls over and touches the electrical outlet (or something similar), over and over.*

ATTUNE	LIMIT SET	PROBLEM SOLVE
You're really interested in that electrical outlet.	It's not for babies. You may not touch that.	Please come back this way. We can play with these balls. *(Or)* I'm going to gently move you to keep you safe.

Note: Babies are testing the world and they can be intrigued when we have a reaction. They can almost seem mischievous, but they are just interested in experimenting and also in our reactions. You may have to repeat this kind of rule over and over, which is normal. Trust that when your baby is ready to believe the limit is being held consistently, she will stop testing it. If your baby continues to try, as if in a loop, you can change the scene by going outside or in another room.

Toddler/Preschooler

SCENARIO: *Getting dressed.*

PREPARATION	ATTUNE	LIMIT SET	PROBLEM SOLVE
In five minutes it will be time to get dressed. *(Five minutes pass.)* Okay, time to get dressed.	Wow, you're really into building that block tower. It's hard to stop, huh?	We do have to get our clothes on now because it's time to leave.	I laid out two outfit choices. Can you guess what they are? Go see them in the other room! Step on whichever outfit you're going to wear. *(Or)* Should we see who can get ready first? I bet I can beat you. *(Or)* I laid out clothes for you—do you want to put them on yourself or should I help you get into them *(follow-through choice)*?

Note: If your child can't yet dress herself, help her get started and let her do the last step.

SCENARIO: *Getting out the door.*

PREPARATION	ATTUNE	LIMIT SET	PROBLEM SOLVE
We're leaving soon to go to school, so everyone do your last thing! In a few minutes we'll put on our shoes and walk out.	You have on socks, but no shoes. I see your backpack still on the hook.	We do have to get on our shoes and leave now, to get there on time.	Who's gonna get their shoes on first, me or you? *(Or)* Anyone want a piggyback ride to the door? *(Or)* What music should we listen to in the car? Do you think you'll have time to play in the yard before school starts? *(Or)* Seems like I need to pick you up and help you *(follow-through choice)*.

SCENARIO: *Coming to the table to eat.*

PREPARATION	ATTUNE	LIMIT SET	PROBLEM SOLVE
We're almost ready to eat. Finish up your last thing and I'll let you know when it's time to come to the table. (*Let him know when dinner is on the table.*)	You don't want to come to the table right now, I get it. *(Or)* I heard you say you're not hungry.	We're going to sit down together for dinner now. You can eat as much as you feel like, but we do always sit together.	Should we crawl like a kitty to the table? *(Or)* I need someone to help me put the napkins on the table. *(Or)* Do you want to come by yourself or should I carry you to the table *(follow-through choice)*?

Note: As soon as your child gets to the table, talk about something interesting, like a bulldozer you saw earlier that day. Don't keep talking about how difficult it was to get him to the table or how frustrated you are.

SCENARIO: *Leaving a fun place.*

PREPARATION	ATTUNE	LIMIT SET	PROBLEM SOLVE
We're going to leave in five minutes. Everyone do your last thing. (*Tell them when time is up.*)	You're sad to say good-bye. It's hard to leave when you're having fun.	We do have to go now.	Should we race to that tree on the way out? I bet I can beat you. (*Or*) Hey, is that Slinky still in the car seat where you left it? Looks like it's hard to leave, so I'm going to help you. Here I come to gently fly you out like a bird (*follow-through choice*).

SCENARIO: *Child throwing a ball in the house.*

ATTUNE	LIMIT SET	PROBLEM SOLVE
I know, it seems like fun to throw in here. (*As you're walking over to the child.*)	Balls are for throwing outside, not in the house.	We can roll it to each other. Wanna play with me? (*If she's not listening, continue.*) We'll put it away for today and play with something else (*follow-through choice*).

School-Age Child

SCENARIO: *You want your child to clean up, but he's not listening.*

ATTUNE	LIMIT SET	PROBLEM SOLVE
Yeah, picking stuff up is not so much fun. I get it. We'd both rather be doing something else in this moment!	It's time to clean up. I'll work on the kitchen while you work on your room. We can help each other with whatever's left over.	Let's get this done so we can go and shoot some hoops. Wanna choose some music to listen to while we clean? Should we race to see who gets their job done first?

SCENARIO: *You need to make a phone call and your child keeps interrupting.*

PREPARATION	ATTUNE	LIMIT SET	PROBLEM SOLVE
I'm about to make a quick phone call.	*(Later, child interrupts when you're on the phone.) Nonverbal: Put your hand on the child's shoulder; make eye contact to let her know you see her.*	When I'm on the phone, I need space. Hold on to your question for a few minutes.	Hand the child a book, and once the call is over, remind her about the limit you set and explain the concept of not interrupting.

Conversations

Leaving the House

I'm noticing the time, and it's ten minutes until we have to leave for piano. Let's see, what are our steps again? We've put clothes on and eaten breakfast, so, hmm, I know there were three steps, I'm just having a hard time rememb—

Brush teeth, brush hair, wash face!

You remember those so well. Jeez, I always forget one. Okay, so do you want to brush your teeth and I'll wet the facecloth, or the other way around?

Your Preschooler Ignores You and Won't Leave School at the End of the Day.

I noticed something and wanted to ask you about it. When I come to pick you up at school, it seems like it's really hard for you to leave. We end up taking a long time and I notice both of us get frustrated!

(Son nods.)

It's hard to leave school at the end of the day?

Yeah, I'm in the middle of playing.

Right, you're in the middle of a project or a game and it's hard to stop, get your lunchbox, and walk out! Okay, so since we do have to get home for dinner, what could we do? What would make it easier?

Give me more time. Today I was playing family with Isla.

I see. What about if, when I arrive, I say hi, and then go to grab your lunchbox and sign you out. While I'm doing that, you'll have a few minutes to do your last thing and pause the game for tomorrow.

Okay.

Then should we meet at the gate after I do the sign-out and you do your last thing?

Yes!

Your Seven-Year-Old Daughter Is Never Ready for School on Time and You're Frustrated.

I see you're still in your pj's and playing with your animals.

(If no progress . . .) Hmm, what time does your clock say? How many more minutes until we have to leave?

Five minutes.

Oh, you're right, five minutes to do the last two things on your chart!

(More time passes . . .) You're a few minutes late for school. What do you do if the bell has already rung?

(Later that day . . .) I could tell you didn't like getting to school late today. You had to get a pass from the office before you could go to your class. Do you have some ideas for how to get ready faster tomorrow? Do you want me to help you write them down?

CHAPTER SIX

Sibling Relationships

*Insisting upon good feelings between the children led
to bad feelings. Acknowledging bad feelings between
the children led to good feelings.*

—**Adele Faber and Elaine Mazlish**

Mara was at a loss and felt like a bad parent. It seemed like her three kids fought, grabbed, name-called, and teased each other constantly. She'd thought, having multiple kids, that they would play together, but instead of playing, they were ready to fight at every turn. If the three-year-old wasn't pinching the baby when the mother's back was turned, the five-year-old was pulling her sister's hair the moment she got frustrated, along with slamming her door and screaming. The baby would cry; the others would sulk; and this went on day after day. It wasn't the happy family Mara had imagined, and she worried about the future of their relationships with each other. She didn't understand why they didn't get along and found herself resorting to yelling and threatening on a daily basis. It felt bad, but she didn't know what else to do. The only thing that seemed to bring peace to the household was to separate the kids.

Sibling Conflicts Turned Opportunities

Sibling conflict tops the list of many parenting challenges. It can be among the most intense, frequent, and seemingly difficult pattern to improve. We hear moms and dads express not only frustration and helplessness but also profound sadness that their kids don't get along. They had envisioned a different kind of family from the one emerging in their homes.

In this chapter, we want to explore and possibly shift your assumptions about why this conflict is so common, while also giving you clear steps and many examples for gradually improving the overall atmosphere in your home. After all the hard work of being a parent, we want you to look forward to reaping more positive results, now and in the future.

The great news is that sibling issues give your kids a chance to practice invaluable life skills. How you help your kids navigate difficult moments with each other will have an impact on their relationships for the rest of their lives. When you use ALP, your kids soak up this way of being and eventually they start to use it with each other. This is a chance to model and practice empathy, and to teach your kids how to ask for empathy from others and to state personal limits: *I'm telling you clearly how I feel and what I think.* Or, *Can you please listen and just let me know you understand me?* Think about how helpful these skills will be with their future partners!

What Causes Sibling Conflict and Rivalry?

Siblings have conflicts for many reasons—and some of these are "good" and healthy. For example:

- Siblings feel secure enough with each other to work out issues of control, leadership, identity, and communicating their needs and feelings.
- Home is a safe place to let big feelings show and to conduct experiments in social dynamics and cause and effect. ("If I say this, what will her reaction be?" "How far can I push this before she snaps?")
- When siblings fight, they're showing their parents that they have a need for guidance, clear rules, family meetings, and other needs covered in chapter 2.
- Big feelings about ownership, territory, and whose turn it is are normal among siblings.
- Children go through developmentally normal stages of a very right or wrong, rigid, or black-and-white. understanding of rules and fairness, which causes friction.
- Conflicts arise based on misunderstandings, often due to age differences.
- Siblings get attention from their parents when they have conflicts.
- Siblings can feel they need to compete for their parents' attention.
- One sibling, often the younger one, wants the attention and company of an older sibling but doesn't know how to get it.

Our clients often have an aha moment or breathe a sigh of relief when we talk about this list, and most of them can add at least one or two more to it. Recently, a mom started to cry during this discussion, as she talked about her two sons. Her older son had always been antagonistic toward the younger one. With his friends he seemed to have endless patience, but with his younger brother he had zero. Everything irritated him and he scorned, teased, and judged every word that came out of the little one's mouth. It was so painful for the mom to hear, and the more she tried to put a lid on it, the worse it got. One day he tripped his little brother and seemed to enjoy seeing him fall down and get hurt. In a fury, the mom took away electronics for a week. This seemed to make him even angrier at his little brother.

We asked her what she was thinking about during our discussion of what causes sibling conflict, and she said that she'd never really tried to look at this from her older son's perspective. Now that she was, she had a few guesses as to what fueled his resentment toward his brother: the little brother needed more help from Mom and Dad because he was younger, he was accomplished in sports, and he often got more attention from visitors and family because he had a happy-go-lucky, easygoing nature. The mother also speculated that, among his friends, her older son was not necessarily a leader, and he might be trying to flex those dominant muscles with his younger sibling.

She didn't have a perfect answer, but she didn't need one. She was thinking below the tip of the iceberg. With this mind-set, over time the tone in the house changed. She came in one day with an accomplishment. There had been a very bad blowup, in which her son had slammed the door on his little brother's arm. Normally she would have yelled, interrogated, and punished her son, but she did not. After making sure her younger one's arm was okay, she took an incredibly long breath, steadied herself, and went into the older one's room. He was on his bed balled up in a fit of rage, so she sat down on the floor, below his level. She put a hand on his back and stroked him for a minute, to let him know she was not there to yell. He started to cry,

"I hate him."

"He made you furious," said Mom.

He kept crying and she gave him more time, using her "good waiter" to paraphrase what he said instead of correcting or fixing. Eventually he got to something closer to the core of the problem, "No one likes me," he said. This made his mom's heart sink, but she held herself back from trying to talk him out of it. "I understand that feeling," she told him.

Over time, in the weeks and months that followed, her son was able to talk more easily, and his mom understood he felt a little threatened by a younger, cuter, more endearing younger brother. The tension in the house went down and they had more fun together.

Enjoying Each Other versus Fighting— What's the Ratio?

Conflict is normal with brothers and sisters. In the same way that kids are often well behaved at school but emotionally fragile and defiant at home, they can skip along brilliantly with friends while they butt heads with their sibling nonstop. We hear that pattern over and over. Almost every parent worries they're doing something wrong.

A certain amount of fighting is healthy, because if it's handled properly, it can bring siblings closer together and allow them to practice conflict resolution. One way to know whether the fighting in your house is healthy or problematic is to look at the proportion of positive to negative interactions between siblings. They should have more instances of playing, laughing, and enjoying each other than they do instances of yelling, tension, and separation. This proportion is more important for their long-term bond than having a completely happy and conflict-free relationship.

So how to turn challenging moments into ones of growth and connection? You know from earlier chapters that your goal is not simply to quiet things down and make conflict go away—if you think this way, your kids will reap only short-term benefits. Your goal is for them to be close and supportive to each other throughout their lives. We'll start by shifting how you perceive siblings' difficult moments.

Creating Positive Beliefs for Your Family to Help Siblings Get Closer

When you think about sibling relationships, what comes to mind? Do you think of them as mostly conflictual and negative, or loving and supportive? Do you emphasize individuality, or togetherness and team building? Are mottoes like "Look out for one another," "Have each other's back," and "Family is precious" explicitly taught in your family? Do you have close relationships with your siblings and see them as precious?

"Oh, they can't stand each other right now" and "They're at each other's throats; they need time apart" are comments we hear from parents a lot. This is a negative assumption about siblings that doesn't help them grow closer. Believe us, we understand the sentiment; if your daughter laughs with an evil twinkle in her eye while your son cries at her meanness, or you hear "Get out of my room," or "I hate you!" it can be hard to see their relationship with a positive view.

The truth is, though, that your children *want* to love each other, share, support each other, and get along. When they have conflicts, it's a normal process of figuring out how to express oneself, how to listen, how to fit one's own needs together with those of another person, and how to problem solve together. For the most part, they do want to be friends—it's our job to help them work through the ups and downs to do this.

Commonly held negative beliefs about siblings (these are not helpful):

- They are not supportive of each other.
- There is constant competition.
- Their fights are silly kid stuff.
- Teasing, making fun, and demeaning are to be expected.
- They have to vie for parents' attention.
- They need to be separated if they fight or argue.

- _____
  _____
- _____
  _____

A more hopeful and helpful set of beliefs about siblings:

- Siblings have special and unique relationships.
- Siblings know each other their whole lives. There is a depth to that history.
- Siblings share a family culture and memories and, of course, a future.
- Siblings support and teach each other.

- Their conflicts deserve respect and their grievances with each other should be taken seriously.
- Working through conflicts feels safer at home with siblings.
- Conflict is always an opportunity to learn something helpful.

- _____
  _____
- _____
  _____

You can take these two lists above and add your ideas to each one. What are your unhelpful beliefs about siblings? What could you add, from your experience and understanding, to the second list of more hopeful and helpful beliefs?

LET THEM HANDLE IT, OR SWOOP IN? SCAFFOLD INSTEAD.

A lot of parents think that kids should be left to work things out on their own—this is how to teach them to be tough and solve their own problems. We do not see it this way at all. In fact, we see it as a missed opportunity. This is a chance to help kids learn and practice conflict resolution, just like any other skill set. In fact, it may be one of the most useful skill sets we can teach them, and this practice can start much younger than most people think.

On the other hand, if we hover or overcontrol, we leave little space for kids to practice their natural empathy and problem-solving skills. When you swoop in with a judgment or solution to a conflict, one or both kids often feels resentful as a result. We will help you find the balance. Your goal is to prompt and assist when needed (a lot, or all the time at first), and over time, kids adopt the language you use and learn to use it with each other. In the beginning, you may need to "get in there" many times every day, using ALP as your guide to asking them the right questions, prompting them to look at each other and say what they want directly, and even giving them the words to say to each other. Over time, they need your help less and less.

This is what psychologists call "scaffolding." Think of yourself, the parent, as scaffolding on a building (the building is your kids). When the building is young and unsteady it needs more support. As the building grows taller and stronger, we gradually take our scaffolding down and give our kids space to navigate these difficult moments on their own. This is a normal developmental process—we don't want to underhelp, nor do we want to overhelp. It's a constant recalibration of this balance. Often parents overhelp (readers of *The Happy Sleeper* will recognize this concept) and are surprised by how capable and ready their kids are to do more (like sleep!) on their own. Even little kids can come up with ideas for how to solve conflicts. They are much more likely to do this if they get the feeling the adults around them value their contribution.

In keeping with these concepts of a positive, healthy vision for siblings and scaffolding conflict resolution, how do we apply our ALP model?

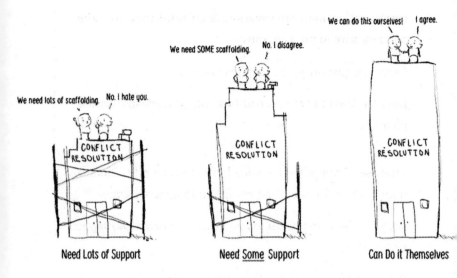

Need Lots of Support   Need <u>Some</u> Support   Can Do it Themselves

Scaffolding gives you a way to help less over time as kids learn how to resolve their own conflicts.

ALP in Sibling Conflicts

Here's a summary of how you can use your attune, limit-setting, and problem-solving steps with sibling conflicts.

ALP FOR SIBLING CONFLICT

Safety: Calmly make sure everyone is safe.

Attune: Help your kids express their feelings to each other or about each other. Let them know you understand and try not to judge or blame. Pause; get on their level; be the sportscaster; gather more information. Wait until they are calm and receptive to problem solve.

I hear you guys are upset, what's happening?

Janie has tears in her eyes and Jack, you're laughing. Someone fill me in.

Limit set: Prompt kids to state limits to each other. State a limit to them if needed and briefly explain the reason.

Tell your sister what you're trying to say in a clear voice so she understands.

We do not hit, because that hurts other people.

Problem solve: Prompt kids to come up with a plan. If they cannot, offer ideas.

Okay, so now, what's your plan?

Yes, that's a toughie. I bet you'll figure it out.

Let's divide the building tiles into two piles so you each know what you're working with.

Safety Step

As with physical behaviors talked about in chapter 4, make sure everyone is safe first before you move to ALP. Depending on the ages of the siblings and on the nuances of the moment, the safety step can be putting a hand between two little heads about to bonk into each other, kindly but firmly holding hitting hands, or telling kids to stop the behavior immediately. Communicate that any physical behaviors (hitting, pushing, kicking, biting, pinching) are 100 percent not okay and your job as a parent is to start by making sure they stop before you do anything else. It's key to stay calm and nonjudgmental. Try this internal mantra (which you can even say out loud at times): "Mommy (or Daddy) will stop you every time until you learn to stop yourself." This reminds you that this approach is a process. Repetition (maybe more than you ever imagined) may be necessary for kids to learn.

Attune

When you're faced with a challenging sibling moment, you will attune to both children, and also help them attune to each other. This is not a one-time trick, in which you can expect your children to gush with understanding for each other instantly. It's a practice and a way of being that builds their awareness of and connection to each other over time.

Sibling grievances can seem really silly. "She got more slices of mango!" "Waaaaa, he beat me to the car!" (Sobbing uncontrollably in the parking lot.) "Get your foot off my side of the couch!" If you put yourself in your kids' shoes, though (or remember your own childhood), these moments are real and genuine. You don't have to wallow in them, but when you acknowledge these feelings, rather than dismissing them, your kids feel taken seriously and understood. You'll have much more success helping them with the limit-setting and problem-solving steps.

Attune Tool #1:
Let Them Be Mad or Sad, and Love Each Other Too

One of our best tools as parents is to let siblings have intense and complicated feelings toward each other. If you try to put a lid on these feelings, they will come out in other ways, like resentment, competition, detachment, physical behaviors, and more. Acknowledge emotions as real, and passing, like the waves in a storm:

"I hate him! He's the meanest brother in the world. I wish he wasn't my brother." What could you say to a child who says this about her sibling?

(Instead of) *Oh, don't say that. You love him. He's your brother!*

(Say) *You sound absolutely furious at him right now.*

Sometimes you want him to just go away. He hurt your feelings really badly.

Parents are often hesitant to do this, but if you let the "negative" feelings be okay, they will eventually pass. Woven into those feelings of anger and fury at a sibling are also feelings of love. If you let the anger run its course, the love and enjoyment will surface again.

Attune Tool #2:
Should You Intervene?

If siblings are in conflict, pause and see if this is a moment for you to intervene or not. If they are mildly bickering, let them be. If you always impose solutions, one or both kids can end up feeling resentful, and they don't get a chance to work it out on their own. Notice the signs that you are needed: Are voices getting louder and more rigid? Is one child yelling louder because the other is not listening? Is one child (or both) tired, hungry, or overstimulated? Resolving conflicts takes a well of patience, and when kids are running low on it, they're more likely to need us to step in. Over time, with practice and your scaffolding, kids become better and better at talking to each other and need your help less. Don't expect this to happen right away, though. There will be many years (or maybe decades!) when you can help them understand each other and communicate. Sometimes you can step in at the most helpful point, early on, to assist and head off a bigger dispute.

If you hear things starting to go south, poke your head in with preemptive attunement:

(Instead of) *Hey, hey, hey, settle down in here. I don't want to hear any more of this.*

(Say) *Do you guys need some help figuring things out?*

Can you give me some information about what's happening?

Attune Tool #3:
The Sportscaster, Good Waiter, and More

The sportscaster is one of the best techniques you can use to help siblings. As you know from chapter 1, the sportscaster observes without judgment and says what is happening, giving the play-by-play. Do not take sides, find blame, or try to shut down communication. Let's imagine you hear voices rising in the other room and you open the door to find one daughter looking confused and guilty, while the other one is screaming, "Take my sweater off. You always do this!"

(Instead of) *If I have to tell you one more time! Why did you take her clothes again?*

(Say) *Okay, Emma, you're really angry. Natalie, you're wearing Emma's sweater and you look like you're not sure what to do next.*

After they've told you what's happened, repeat it back (paraphrase, as in the good waiter) without solving it for them,

So, Natalie, you're saying you really wanted to wear it and you thought if you asked, she'd say no. It seemed better just to do it. Emma, you love that sweater and worry it will get dirty. I see. I get why this was a tough one. Am I missing anything?

If you start this way, your kids can begin to hear each other and work out a solution. Try to paraphrase for them before jumping in with your own ideas. See if they can problem solve on their own.

The investigative reporter technique. If you didn't see what happened, then, without bias, imagine you're just appearing on the scene and your role is to collect information about both kids. You can even be the head-scratching, bumbling parent and act a little confused and unsure.

(Instead of) *Hey, Natalie, what did you do now?*

(Say something like) *Ooh, what's happening here?*

Whoa, I hear this. Can you both help me understand?

Can you guys tell me about this?

Let's back up. Can you fill me in?

Think out loud. Make your process of understanding them transparent—this helps your kids learn, and it also keeps you all on the same team.

We might have to take a few deep breaths before we can understand this better.

I can see why you guys got stuck here.

Hm, let me think for a minute—I want to listen to both of you.

"CUT IT OUT!"

"Hey, cut it out, settle down, be nice, stop yelling, don't be mean." These phrases are so easy to say, but they are dismissive and don't teach kids anything about what *to* do. Instead, say an attune phrase like "What's happening here?" "Let me understand this," or "Your voices are rising."

Attune Tool #4:
Show Equal Empathy, Even to the "Perpetrator"

This may be one of the trickiest parts of helping siblings resolve conflicts: to see the "victim" and the "perpetrator" each with equal kindness and curiosity. The one who, in a traditional sense, would be labeled the perpetrator is sometimes the one who needs your empathy and guidance more. It doesn't mean you will excuse misbehavior or breaking rules.

"I get so mad at Aiden for provoking and teasing his sister that I yell at him and send him to time-out constantly—he's out of control!" A mom shared this with us on the topic of siblings. As we talked, she realized, first of all, that she didn't intervene early enough—her kids needed more scaffolding. She was hoping they would work it out and left it too long before helping. But she also realized that Aiden needed more empathy, not more punishments. Yelling at him was making it worse—giving him the reputation of the "difficult" one, making him feel resentful and more likely to act out toward his sister.

One afternoon, she heard her daughter start to whine miserably. She poked her head in to watch and saw that Aiden was having a grand old time teasing her about her braces, and he seemed to enjoy seeing her eyes well up with tears. She remembered what it was like to be teased herself. She instantly felt angry and wanted to yell, "Hey, go to your room right now. That is not okay! Time-out!" Instead, she got closer to them and said, *Aiden, your sister looks pretty sad about whatever it is you're saying to her* (sportscaster). She squatted down between them and put a hand on both of them. *Can you tell me what's happening* (investigative reporter)? Aiden seemed unremorseful, which irritated her. But she also knew she hadn't seen him all day and realized this "bad behavior" was the reason for their first real conversation (iceberg analogy). *We don't name-call because that hurts people's feelings* (limit). *I know I've been on the computer since you guys got home from school. . . . I'm wondering if you're missing our time when we hang out together and have a snack?* (problem solve).

It turned out she was right. Aiden needed a moment of down-time with his mom after not seeing her all day. The rest of the afternoon, she didn't hear him provoke his sister at all. Mom continued working on using the attune step in this way and Aiden's relationship with his sister gradually improved. At first Mom was worried about being indulgent, but she didn't excuse the teasing. By intervening sooner, she helped Aiden understand himself better. He learned that he didn't need to "act out" his feelings—he could ask for what he needed directly. Having his sister witness all of this also helped her have more empathy for what was really going on with him.

Staying neutral as much as possible will help kids not feel un-fairly blamed. For example, one sibling may be more physically aggressive, so she may be the one who gets blamed for doing something wrong. But was she provoked by her sister's verbal aggression? Some kids are adept at mentally provoking their siblings, causing the siblings to act out in a more obvious way. Do your best to approach each situation with an open mind. This is something we practice in all of our relationships and it can be most challenging when faced with a sibling spat.

Let's take a typical sibling clash: Julia and Colin are playing in their bedroom. All of a sudden, the mom hears a thump, and one kid starts to cry. The mom runs in to see Julia standing there holding a toy phone and Colin holding his head and crying. When they see their mom, Julia starts to cry and drops the phone, and Colin cries even harder.

What should the mom do? She'd be pretty justified in assuming Julia smacked her brother over the head with the phone, so we wouldn't be surprised if she said something like, *Julia, what did you do? No hitting your brother!*

Instead, she takes a different approach. She goes over to both kids, gets on their level, and holds Colin in her arm while touching Julia with her other hand. *Whoa, are you okay? Let me see your head,* she says to Colin as she makes sure he's okay. *What happened?* she says to both kids, while still touching them and being on their level. Her body language and touch make Julia feel like she isn't shaming or judging her, so she shares information. *He wasn't playing my game,* says Julia. *Ah, you wanted to play a certain game, and Colin had a different idea? You got frustrated and hit him with the phone* (good waiter)? Now the mom has more facts. *I see. Remember our family rule about being safe with each other's bodies,* she says. *Check in with Colin and let's see if he needs an ice pack.*

Attune Tool #5:
Help Your Kids Attune to Each Other

This is a hugely valuable skill to teach your kids. Eventually, it will become their go-to way of dealing with difficult moments. Help each of the siblings see the issue from the other's perspective. Ask questions that point them toward empathy for the other.

I can see she's having some feelings about this. What do you think is going on?

Why do you think he did that?

Can you tell her what you're thinking about right now?

He looks sad—I wonder why. Do you know?

Tell her how that made you feel.

Can you ask him to please listen to how you feel?

FROM HEATHER

My kids have been practicing resolving their own little conflicts, with our scaffolding, since they were toddlers. People
would laugh at us because sometimes it sounded like we
expected way too much from a two-year-old. *Can you tell him
your idea? What are you trying to say to him? Say it in a clear
voice. What's your plan for figuring this out?* . . . But one day I
heard them in their bedroom starting to get frustrated and
one yelled at the other, "You're upset? Okay, well, tell me your
idea!"

Attune Tool #6:
Compare in a Helpful Way

It's so tempting to compare your kids to each other. You may think,
How better for them to learn than if I point out how well or how
badly their sibling is performing? "Can't you just finish your homework and do it neatly, like your sister does?" "Your brother is helping
and you're not!" "She's my easy child. Her sister is another story."
This contributes to siblings feeling competitive or resentful of each
other. Instead, see each of your children as unique and able individ-
uals who need your guidance when they're not doing so well as their

siblings. Kids need to be shown that everyone is on their unique path to learning and developing skills.

Jackie is still learning about not hitting.

Ben just learned to walk so he hasn't learned to run yet.

There are so many types of "smarts," aren't there?

Danny, do you remember when you started playing this game and it was frustrating to you? What do you think would help Louise?

Kids naturally compare themselves to each other. Jack was a dad of two who was trying to help his daughter relax about learning to read. She had an avid reader for an older brother and now that she was in kindergarten, she was coming home saying things like "I'll never learn to read. I'm the worst reader in the world. I'm the worst sister in the world." When Jack said, "What? That's crazy, you're great! Don't worry, you're so smart. Soon you'll be reading just like your brother," she seemed to sulk even more and say she didn't want to try. He was missing a chance to attune. We suggested he try a different framework for differences: *It's a challenge, this learning to read stuff, isn't it? It feels frustrating in the beginning. Did you know that it's not really important how fast you read, but it's more important to let your brain enjoy the workout? You'll find different ideas and solve different puzzles in a book than your brother—that's the beauty of reading.*

WELCOMING DIFFERENCES; APPRECIATING DIVERSITY

<u>Julie:</u> When I was a kid, my parents used to say to me and my siblings, "Comparisons are odious." How funny is that? This proverb dates back to the fifteenth century. It means that we should not make comparisons between two people, because it is very likely unjust to one or both, and can be divisive. We won't use the word "odious," but sometimes old sayings are truly wise.

While comparing is a developmentally normal thing to do, we, as parents, can actively teach our children not to do it, or at least *how* to do it. You'll hear your kids start to compare. "He's better than me," "I can run faster than you." "I got a 100 on my spelling test and you didn't!" "She's prettier than me." It goes on and on. Comparing often makes one person feel bad or "less than," and it doesn't open young minds to accepting and valuing differences. Instead, we can help our kids to be curious and appreciative of diversity in thought, background, physical appearance, abilities, and so forth:

What an interesting world we live in—everyone is different. How boring would it be if everyone was exactly the same?

Everyone's bodies are different in their shapes, sizes, and colors.

We all have things that feel easy and things we have to work harder at. Everyone is learning all the time.

Each person thinks differently and has unique ideas. We can learn from each other.

Children will express a natural curiosity about people who are different from them. These moments are opportunities for parents to model not just accepting, but embracing, differences.

When feelings are intense, one or both kids are overloaded, (and you're not in a public place where the behavior is disruptive), stay in the attune step and give them time to get their feelings out and ride the bigger wave of the storm before you move on to the limit-setting and the problem-solving step. As long as everyone is safe and not destroying anything, taking this time is exactly what they need. These episodes, to little kids, can literally feel like the end of the world. They need to know we understand and will stay nearby until they are calmer and open to talking and figuring things out.

Sometimes the attune step will do it. If your kids seem reconciled and find a resolution on their own or go back to playing or hanging out without friction, you're done. Especially if you're certain they are fully aware of the limit or family rule, there's no need for you to repeat it. Once they know the rules, it really helps to let them know that we know they know. If you know what we mean!

If, on the other hand, a rule is still being broken or the squabble is continuing, you will move right on to the limit-setting step.

Limit Set

With siblings, limit setting goes in multiple directions. You, as a parent, will state a limit to your children. The bonus—and where the real beauty and opportunity lies in sibling conflicts—is to teach them to state their own limits to each other.

Limit-Setting Tool #1:
Help Siblings Set Limits with Each Other

As with the attune step, you want to also teach your kids how to use the limit-setting step with each other. Learning and practicing how to set personal limits and boundaries in a calm, confident, and kind way is an incredible relationship skill for life. So many of us can relate to this, as we can tend to get angry or resentful when our limits are being challenged, instead of simply being clear and self-possessed.

Depending on your kids' ages and skill levels, look for opportunities to help them state their own limits to each other. If they can do it in a spirit of really communicating their needs, it will increase their understanding of each other and, in turn, their mutual empathy will grow. This is how the ratio of positive to negative moments with each other will increase.

In the case of Aiden teasing his sister about her braces, we asked the mom how she could coach her daughter to set limits in a way that Aiden could really hear them, rather than just whining and getting upset. She had great ideas for what her daughter could tell him when he started teasing her:

You're teasing me and that's not okay. It hurts my feelings.

I'm going in the other room. I'm not playing with you if you're teasing me. It's not fun.

Just as we're asking you to tell kids what you *do* want, you can teach them to do the same with one another. This is an incredibly helpful skill—teaching children to stand up for what they think and want, and to have clear boundaries. It also turns around the bickering, whining, and complaining a lot of parents witness between siblings.

WHEN YOU SAY . . .

Okay, now tell her what you DO want.

Let him know what you're thinking.

What are you trying to tell him?

Did you have a different idea—what was it?

Let's ask him what he wanted.

IT WILL HELP THEM SAY TO EACH OTHER . . .

I'm not okay with that game.

This is too rough!

Your body is too close to me.

I need space.

I was working with that and I'm not done.

Can I please have a turn after you?

I don't like that—please stop.

Name-calling hurts my feelings.

I want to play my own game for a while, then we can play together.

Tell me what you want, not what you don't want, please!

Limit-Setting Tool #2:
Use the "I Know You Guys Know This, But . . ." Tone

State the family agreements and rules with an "I know you guys totally know this rule already" tone of voice. We believe in our kids and want to interact with them assuming the best—assuming they have good intentions, know the rules, and will follow them (they just need help navigating and reminders).

You guys know that hitting is never okay. Tell her how you feel with words.

Right, and we know we don't throw toys, so . . .

Well, and since we park our toys and screens while we're eating . . .

So, hmm, we don't name-call. I think what you're trying to say is . . .

Problem Solve

Problem-Solving Tool #1:
Invite Suggestions with "Can You Come Up with a Plan?"

Prompt your kids to problem solve with each other. Say something like

Okay, so what plan could you guys have?

I bet you guys will figure out what to do next. I'm here if you get stuck.

Use your head-scratching, bumbling parent stance here.

Hmm, okay, so now that we know the rules, I wonder—what could you do instead?

So you guys are each giving me information. Now, Mary, what do you think the solution could be?

Joey, what's your idea for what to do now?

As long as the plans and ideas your kids come up with are safe and everyone agrees, follow their lead and let them be the ones to own the plan. Often little kids move on and drop the toy they were playing with or forget about the once-contentious dilemma altogether. That's okay, it's the precedent of sharing ideas and problem solving in the moment that is important.

FROM HEATHER: THE DOLLHOUSE FORTRESS

My kids were playing together one morning and my son had set up a "battle" game with a fleet of figures in the living room. Slowly, my daughter started losing interest and saying she didn't want to play this game anymore and that she was going to play with her dollhouse. I had the feeling that they actually *wanted* to play together in that moment, but that she wasn't engaged anymore because her ideas weren't being heard. I started to sportscast for them and ask questions like "It seems like you have a different plan—can you share your thoughts?" and "This is a puzzle, huh, because you want to play dollhouse, and you're really into this battle." I didn't propose a solution, I just paraphrased. Before I knew it, the dollhouse was incorporated into the battle scene and used as the fortress for the figures! Each of them needed to give their ideas life and a little help fitting them together into the same game.

Problem-Solving Tool #2:
Redirect with "Hey, Look Over There!"

Are your kids just caught in a stuck moment? Is one or both hungry, bored, tired? We don't want you to avoid conflicts or just smooth things over, but sometimes kids just need our help shifting the energy. A change of scenery or just good old-fashioned distraction works wonders, especially with babies and little kids. If you notice tension rising, sometimes you can catch it before it gets out of control.

Announce it's smoothie-making time, everyone report to the kitchen.

Move bodies, go outside to run around, get the wiggles out, and get fresh air.

Put on music—a soundtrack can change everything.

Have an impromptu dance party.

Give your kids a common project, goal, or task:

> *Oh, I super duper need help loading those twigs into that bucket over there . . .*

> *You know what would be amazing? I don't know if you guys can do this, but is there any way you could line up all those blocks to reach from one side of the room to the other? I wonder what that would look like.*

Problem-Solving Tool #3:
Checking In Instead of Saying Sorry

As described in chapter 4, saying sorry is just fine, but there are more helpful ways to support empathy and help your kids reconnect with each other. Say something that directs one child's attention to the other's thoughts and feelings or suggests a way to help the other person.

Check in with Mary. I see she's looking sad.

Ask him if he needs anything.

Come with me and we'll get an ice pack for Henry.

When your body is feeling more calm, check in with your sister.

(Checking in when someone's body or feelings are hurt can be a family agreement. See page 195.)

Remember the repair-and-circle-back step from chapter 1? The same ideas apply here. We don't have to sweep conflict under the rug and just pray it doesn't happen again—let your kids see that you're comfortable talking about it.

Hey, you guys, I was thinking about what happened yesterday. I have an idea and want your thoughts too.

Do you guys feel better about what happened? How did you figure it out?

Remember to wait until the storm has passed before you repair. In the midst of high tensions and emotional floods, information will not be received and integrated well, so this isn't the time to teach.

"PLAY NICE!"
PEER RELATIONSHIPS AND SOCIAL SKILLS

Many of the concepts in this chapter apply to conflicts that arise at the park or on playdates, at school, and in other social situations. The major difference is that your family rules only apply to *your* family, and how your own kids behave out in the world. You can't really affect the behavior of a nonsibling playmate. Peer conflicts are a great opportunity for this reason—for your kids' whole lives, there will always be people in the world who don't have the same ideas as they do, people who do things they don't like or understand.

Attune

Conflicts with friends and classmates are a chance to guide kids toward being curious, instead of reactive. We can prompt kids to look beneath the surface with peers:

Emily talked to you in a way you really didn't like, huh? I wonder what was going on with her today.

I know Mark was upset about losing the game. Do you think that's why he said you messed up?

Did you know that Jake just moved here? It's not easy making all new friends.

Rene sometimes is really quiet at the beginning of the day. She just needs time.

Limit Set

When peer conflicts arise, you may need to state a limit or a reality. Prompt your children to state their own limits and boundaries to friends, state their wishes, and get their ideas across.

What could you tell her so she understands your idea clearly?

We can't control what other people do. But we can control what we decide to do.

Could you tell her in a loud, strong voice to stop?

Give her that information.

Do you want to let her know you were working with that?

Problem Solve

Your child could propose a solution, or when the other child is not open to resolving the conflict, her choices will include walking away, taking a break, and staying calm, even while holding her ground. This nonreactive behavior can really defuse these conflicts and kids end up feeling capable and in charge, instead of like the victim.

A client of ours shared how she helped her preschool-age daughter speak up for herself. One evening at dinner, her daughter told her a friend had taken the blocks and pushed her out of the way. Her daughter has a gentle nature, so Mom and daughter practiced advocating for yourself, using what they called the "strong voice." Mom had to encourage her to really speak up, in a clear and loud way, to get the message across, and they role-played it:

> *Mom: Let's practice that strong voice right now. Pretend I'm Sammy and I've just taken the blocks from you.*
> *Daughter: I don't like being pushed! I'm playing with the blocks now.*

The same applied when she started playing sports—they practiced bumping into people and holding your ground. Now as an elementary schooler, she's a super confident kid who speaks up for herself.

If bullying is occurring, it's a good idea to find out what

the policies are at the school or other facility regarding bullying and make sure your child knows about them. Often kids are being bullied and they don't know what to do. As with other difficult subjects, talk about bullying openly before a problem arises. What it is, what it looks like, and what to do about it. It's also possible that your child is the one doing the bullying. In this case, use the tools in this chapter to look beneath the tip of the iceberg, while also firmly and consistently holding limits on the behaviors. You will also have to guide the process of repair. It's especially challenging to us as parents when our child is the "perpetrator." Be kind to yourself, be ready to attune first, and know that you have an effective ALP plan handy.

Problem-Solving Tool #4: Reframe, "No Fair!"

Each child needs your empathy, but they won't all have exactly the same needs, limits, or outcomes. Your older child may have a later bedtime or be allowed to use the sharp knife to cut food. One child may need more one-on-one attention to do homework. One child may get a Popsicle after a doctor visit, much to the devastation of the other, who later sees the wrapper. Little kids can often get caught up in things being exactly the same. Rather than making sure each child has equal toys or exactly the same treatment, address each child's individual needs as a separate person. You'll help and respond to each of them in their unique way.

You two are different people. Different ideas, wants, and needs.

When you're younger, your body is growing so much that you need more sleep. Your brother needs ten hours of sleep at night and your body needs twelve.

Yes, your brother needed something cold to eat after the doctor's office. That was something that happened just to him today. Hey, it was kind of like when you and I stopped at the doughnut shop after getting a flu shot!

PREPARING YOUR CHILD FOR A NEW BABY

A new sibling can be a big adjustment for some kids, and it's not just the few weeks surrounding the birth—the ripple effects of a new sibling can last years. It changes the family forever. If you need help seeing this from your child's perspective, imagine what it would be like to come home introducing your husband to the "new addition"—a second husband.

You're going to love him.

I have enough love for both of you.

He'll be your new brother and you can teach him things.

These would all miss the mark, wouldn't they? The point is to empathize with how it *truly* feels to your older child to have an addition to the family.

Our family feels different now that the baby is here. Daddy's still getting used to it too.

It's not so easy taking care of a baby, is it? I wish I had more time to play with you.

I miss you—I could use some snuggles while I feed
the baby.

You can set the sibling relationship on the right foot with how you talk to the older brother or sister about the new addition.

Before the Baby Arrives

- Tell your older child about when she was born and what she was like as a baby. Explain how you took care of her and all the things she couldn't do then that she can do now.

- Make her a book, using pictures and simple sentences, telling the story of her life from birth to the present day. Leave blank pages at the end to add new events, including the arrival of the baby.

- Display her baby photos in your home where she can see them.

- Read storybooks about the addition of a new baby to the family and what babies are like.

- If your child is interested, get her a baby doll for pretend play and show her how you held her and soothed her when she was tiny.

- Take her to a prenatal visit. If possible, let her listen to the baby's heartbeat and maybe see him moving and kicking in the ultrasound.

- Sing and talk together to your baby.

- Try to avoid moving her from her crib to a bed right before the baby arrives.

- Explain the plan for when you go to the hospital.

- You can have your child help you pack your bag for the hospital and include a toy for the new baby.

- Let her express all feelings about the new baby. Empathize with those feelings and don't try to correct or talk her out of them.

After the Baby Is Born

- Have a quiet family moment when you bring the baby home for the first time.

- If you can put the baby down before your child walks in to meet him for the first time, you will have your arms open to greet your older child, then meet the new baby together.

- Invite your child to "help" you with the new baby (hand you a diaper; talk, read, and sing to him; or help you figure out what he needs). Be careful not to treat her like a little parent, though; she still needs to be a child.

- If your child is too rough, use ALP to help her learn to touch and hold the baby gently, rather than reprimanding or saying "Don't touch." (See script on page 272 with Naomi and her baby brother.)

- There are many parts of your daily routine that you can do with both kids (reading books, taking a bath, playing, or going on outings). You can read to your child while you are feeding the baby or have her play nearby with you looking on.

- Find time to play alone with your child for at least thirty minutes every day, if possible. She needs these intervals to reconnect and reestablish trust and a secure bond with you, considering this profound change in your family.

- Allow your child to have mixed feelings about the baby and empathize with how she feels. You can even share her feelings on some level.

- Every now and then, tell the baby he needs to wait (as you will often need to say to your older child): *Wait a minute, baby. I'll be right there. Ruby and I are getting pj's on and we'll be right back to help you in a sec.*

- It's very normal for your child's behavior to temporarily

regress. Potty training may stall, bedtime can get rocky, and she may even want to drink milk from a bottle again. Without a big reaction from you, let this be okay. It will pass if you don't label it in a negative way.

Scripts and Conversations

Scripts

Baby and Toddler

SCENARIO: *Will is pinching his baby sister when Mom and Dad aren't watching.*

SAFETY	ATTUNE	LIMIT SET	PROBLEM SOLVE
While you're still learning about not pinching, I'm going to keep you two nearby so I can keep everyone safe.	Will, I understand. It's so different having a new baby sister, isn't it? It's hard for you when I have to take care of her.	It's not okay to pinch. Pinching hurts people's bodies.	When you feel mad or sad about your sister, you can tell me. Say, "Mommy, I'm sad." I will always listen to you. And, if you want, you can pinch some Play-Doh to get your mad feelings out. Come on, I'll do it with you!

SCENARIO: *Lilly tells her dad, "I wish I were a baby . . ."**

ATTUNE	PROBLEM SOLVE
Seems fun to just be carried around everywhere? You want to be fed and taken care of like your little brother? That'd be nice.	Did you know I used to swaddle you with . . . lemme just show you with this blanket from the couch . . . see, I'd wrap it like this . . .

* No limit setting is needed in this scenario.

SCENARIO: *Your seven-month-old baby starts pulling his twin brother's hair. The brother starts to cry.*

ATTUNE	LIMIT SET	PROBLEM SOLVE
Oh, Evan, I saw that Wesley pulled your hair. That didn't feel good. Are you okay? Wesley, you were trying to touch Evan's hair? It looks like a fun thing to touch.	We have to touch hair gently or else it hurts.	Let me take your hand and show you how to touch Evan's hair gently. You can also touch my hair gently. Look, Evan is smiling! That feels better to him.

SCENARIO: *Naomi, your two-year-old, is playing too roughly with her four-month-old brother. The baby gets upset.*

ATTUNE	LIMIT SET	PROBLEM SOLVE
Naomi, I see you wanting to hold and play with your little brother.	Let's always use our gentle touch so we don't hurt each other.	I will show you how to touch and hold the baby gently. Let's practice lots of ways to touch gently. His arm, his hair, his toes, your toes, my toes! Aw, can you see that he likes gentle touch?

SCENARIO: *Cassie, nine months old, and Ethan, her two-year-old brother, are playing on the floor. Cassie starts grabbing a ball from Ethan, who starts to yell.*

ATTUNE	LIMIT SET	PROBLEM SOLVE
Hmm, let me see if I can figure this out. Ethan was playing with the ball and Cassie wanted to play with it too. She can't talk yet so she just started grabbing it. You both really wanted to hold the ball!	When Cassie's a little older, she'll be ready to learn about not grabbing. Now she is learning that when she grabbed the ball from you, it made you feel sad and mad. That will help her understand how it makes you feel. When you were Cassie's age, you didn't know about not grabbing yet and you couldn't talk yet.	Let's find another ball so you can each hold one. Cassie will probably still want the one you're holding, Ethan. You can keep trading with her. Little babies are so funny, aren't they? Or we can go outside for a little while and throw the balls back and forth.

SCENARIO: *Ten-month-old Oliver has started biting his two-year-old sister, Abigail, when he feels frustrated or excited.*

SAFETY	ATTUNE	LIMIT SET	PROBLEM SOLVE
Let's move you apart a little so we can be safe. Oliver, I'm going to scoot you back this way a little. Abigail, let me see your arm. Do you want a cool pack for it?	Oliver, you were frustrated that you couldn't reach your sister's toy (or excited when she came home from preschool).	Biting is never okay, because it hurts people. I am going to stop you every time.	Here's a teether that you *can* bite. Or you can give your teddy bear a big hug. Maybe Abigail would like a hug too. Open your arms and see if she does!

SCENARIO: *Gary really wants to play with his baby brother, but he's being too rough and swinging the stroller around too wildly.*

ATTUNE	LIMIT SET	PROBLEM SOLVE
Whoa, buddy, let me help you with the stroller! You want to give your brother a fun ride?	We can give him a fun ride, but we also have to make sure the stroller doesn't tip over so he stays safe. You're practicing how to push him safely.	Let's practice together, pushing the stroller. Can we go in a big circle to make it fun for him, but not too fast? Or you can walk in front of him and make funny faces. Look, he's laughing, he loves it!

Toddler and School-Age Child

SCENARIO: *Luke wants to play with his older sister, Maddie. She dismisses him and he provokes her to try to get her to play. She finally loses it—she starts calling him names and saying "You're a stupid head." Luke starts to cry.*

ATTUNE	LIMIT SET	PROBLEM SOLVE
I hear one person calling names in an angry voice, and another person is crying. Let me see. Maddie, you wanted space, huh, and got mad when Luke kept trying?	In our family we don't call each other names. How could you give him that information in a clear way without calling him names?	Okay, so, hmm, what's the plan? *(Wait. If they need more scaffolding . . .)* Maddie, how about letting Luke know when you're ready to play together again? Luke, since she asked for space, what's your plan? You and I could practice our cartwheels. Or you could keep building your Lego airport . . .

SCENARIO: *The older brother says his little sister gets more help.*
"You never let me do that!" "You always do things for her." "You
never make her clean up her dishes . . ."

ATTUNE	REALITY*	PROBLEM SOLVE
Seeing your sister without as many responsibilities feels unfair. We help her more than you, huh?	She does need a bit more help, it's true. You were just the same when you were her age. Now you can do all kinds of things that she can't yet. Your help makes a big difference in our family.	After we clean up, wanna look at some baby videos of you? It will probably help you feel better and understand your sister if you see what a little guy you used to be!

* The reality step is in place of the limit setting, because no limit applies in this scenario.

SCENARIO: *The kids are vying for your attention. They're putting*
on a talent show and one keeps hogging the limelight.

ATTUNE	LIMIT SET	PROBLEM SOLVE
I love this talent show, but I'm only seeing one performer. Marcus, you are really loving this, aren't you? Check in with Sara, because she looks a little frustrated, like she'd like a turn.	Sara, let him know in a clear, strong voice that you want a turn.	What's the plan?

SCENARIO: *"That's not fair! How come he got an ice cream after school and I didn't?"*

ATTUNE	REALITY	PROBLEM SOLVE
You saw Rex with the ice cream and felt left out. I know the feeling.	Rex had a tough day at school today and we decided to get ice cream together and talk about it. Sometimes I do this kind of thing with you, like a few weeks ago when we stopped for a smoothie on the way home from your swimming class. Remember, you were so hungry?	Mommy and I don't always do the same things with you guys. You are each different people and have different things going on. We also sometimes like to have special time with each of you and then you can choose what you want to do.

SCENARIO: *Your older, more rational child is building paper airplanes. The younger, tornado-like child destroys them.*

ATTUNE	LIMIT SET	PROBLEM SOLVE
Oh, man, Evelyn, I know you worked hard making all of your paper airplanes. You had quite a fleet of them. Leah crushed them and you're mad. Leah, I think you were curious and didn't know how fragile they are. Am I missing anything?	Leah, I'm going to make it a rule for now that you don't touch Evelyn's airplanes. The reason is that they are too delicate and fragile to play with.	Hmm, what could we do? *(Wait. If they need more scaffolding . . .)* Maybe we could help Leah make some very simple paper airplanes of her own and then she can do whatever she wants with those. And what would you think of keeping yours up on this shelf where she can't reach them?

Conversations

My Piano Teacher

Abby wasn't expecting to have a chance to practice her ALP skills when she told her nine-year-old son, Harry, that his younger brother, Liam, was going to start taking piano lessons with the same teacher Harry had been studying with for a few years. To her surprise, Harry fell apart and cried, inconsolably, in her arms for twenty minutes. Abby resisted the urge to judge, dismiss, or jolly away Harry's feelings. She stayed curious and after some time passed, Harry was finally able to explain.

Miss Jasmine is my teacher. I don't want to share her.

You feel like she's just for you and not for Liam?

Yes, it's like it's my thing only I get to do and I really like Miss Jasmine.

So maybe, if Liam took lessons from her too, it wouldn't feel so special?

Yeah.

I understand exactly what you mean. It's hard to think about sharing someone you've spent so much happy time with. You've also worked hard and learned a lot from her.

I know.

Did I tell you that Miss Jasmine told me she really loves teaching you? She said that you have a wonderful feeling when you play and also that it means a lot to her that you take your practicing so seriously.

She did?

She did.

Huh, well, Liam will have to start with the same beginner's music that I did.

You're right, he will.

Abby didn't have to do any more. Harry recovered and, going forward, was fine about Liam starting lessons. All he needed was to be seen and heard and understood.

CHAPTER SEVEN

Screen Time

They feel compelled to confess their sins of how much television their children watch.

—Dr. Dimitri Christakis

When we introduce the topic of screens in our parenting groups (even with moms and dads of the littlest babies) the discussion brims with concerns and questions. Is it okay to let babies watch a thirty-minute show? How much screen time is healthy for toddlers? How can you avoid power struggles and meltdowns with a video-game-obsessed child?

Media and screens are now part of our kids' daily lives in an unprecedented way. The technologies to watch and play are ever growing, as are the devices geared to the youngest viewers (we've even seen potties, changing tables, and cribs adorned with screens). Everywhere you go, you see babies playing with their parents' cell phones. American toddlers and little kids have roughly two hours of screen time a day. As kids grow, so does their time spent with screens: On any given day, American tweens (eight- to twelve-year-olds) use an average of six hours' worth of entertainment media, and that's excluding time spent at school or for homework (when many are multitasking, doing homework while connecting on social media or playing video games at the same time). Teenagers average nine hours of entertainment media use.

READING FOR PLEASURE DECLINES WITH AGE

Research suggests a drop-off in reading for pleasure as kids grow. Approximately half of nine-year-olds read for pleasure, whereas only 19 percent of teens read for pleasure. For comparison, in the 1980s, the same percentage of nine-year-olds read for pleasure, but 30 percent of teens did.

Rather than thinking of screens as good or bad, in this chapter we'll look at the question in a more nuanced and helpful way. It's not just the amount of time spent on screens that matters, it's also how technology is integrated into family life, what the family habits are (including parents'), what specific programs children are watching and games they're playing, and how we talk to them about all of this. Our goal here is to briefly look at the research and clinical thinking on media and screens, use this as a starting point for creating family agreements and habits, and give you scripts and examples of how to talk to kids about screens and troubleshoot common stuck moments. We don't want you to feel worried or guilty about screens, we want to empower you to be mindful of how your family uses them—to be in control of devices rather than letting them control you.

Screens, Family Relationships, and Health

"Hey, Mom and Dad, Over Here!"
Devices and Parent–Child Interactions

Recently, we watched a well-meaning dad and his kids out for dinner and saw the pitfalls of technology and parenting in action. Dad and the kids started out chatting, but soon the dad's phone beckoned him. He looked at it over and over. Toward the middle of the meal, the kids started bickering. The dad laid his phone down on the table and said, "Hey, no name-calling or we're leaving. Stop it." A few minutes later, he was back on his phone. Soon the kids were fighting, standing on the benches and running around the restaurant. The dad took out another device and all three family members ended up on electronics until dinner was over. No one looked happy with the way the meal turned out.

This is an example we can all relate to in one way or another. For many of us, our devices are on hand at all times. Work correspondence, social connections, calendars, sports, photos—we engage with our devices (often with good reason) every day, nonstop. Research suggests adults, just like teens, spend an average of nine hours per day looking at screens—the majority of which is not work related.

We tend to think of screens as a kid issue, but if we want to raise smart screen consumers, the first place to start is with ourselves. Whether we're doing extensive research or quickly checking a message, our children (even our babies) pick up on our continual interest in and reliance on our devices. The problem is that, in excess, it disrupts a natural back-and-forth of interaction, eye contact, and response that is so critical to children's development. Babies and kids learn about the world with us as their guides, so when we're available, they learn more. When we look at them with genuine curiosity and don't rush them, they feel understood. This is harder and harder to do when our devices and electronics are constantly pinging and our attention is being pulled away. Indeed, research suggests that screens distract parents and disrupt moment-to-moment interactions in the family, and that parents and children interact less when parents have access to their mobile devices.

... AND THEN WE CAN PLAY DRAGON TREASURE HUNTERS AND ...

Of course, we don't need science to tell us that screens are distracting. Most of us feel this and many of us are already concerned and trying to make more conscious choices about screens for ourselves. In the next section, you'll see ideas for setting limits for *you* and talking about devices and screens in a way that will help your child interact with screens in a healthy and smart way.

Screens and Sleep

The research on screens and sleep is clear: Watching screens, particularly in the evening, is associated with delayed bedtimes, less sleep, and poorer quality sleep overall. Children with screens in their bedroom sleep less and are more likely to have a sleep problem. Babies exposed to screens in the evenings at the age of six to twelve months sleep less overall than those not exposed to evening screens, and each additional hour of evening media use for preschoolers is associated with a significant increase in sleep problems. Kids who are on a screen in the ninety minutes before bed are more likely to have a later sleep time.

For school-age kids, sleeping near a small screen, sleeping with a TV in the room, and having more screen time overall are associated with shorter sleep durations.

Why are screens at odds with our kids' sleep? There are a number of reasons:

- Electronic screens emit light that sends alerting signals to the brain. Light from many electronic devices is blue—which on the electromagnetic spectrum is similar to sunlight. In the evenings, an hour or two before our bodies are ready to fall asleep, the drowsy-making hormone melatonin begins to rise. Light suppresses the release of melatonin, making us less likely to fall asleep at our optimal bedtime. This applies to toddlers, school-age children, teenagers, and parents—the impact of light on sleep is a powerful universal human phenomenon.

- Content can be activating to the brain. An interactive game or another screen-based activity requires kids to be engaged, make decisions, receive rewards or not, advance to the next level or not—all of which keeps the brain awake, releases stress hormones, and makes it harder to disengage and fall asleep. If your little one is dodging fireballs or slaying dragons, his brain will be looping this mental activity, and his body will still be feeling it when he closes his eyes.

- Screens become a point of negotiation, which can lead to emotional outbursts and delay bedtime routines. It's hard for kids to turn off screens (even harder than it is for us), so watching screens before bed can often snowball into power struggles, while early bedtimes slide later.

Health and Development

The research on how screens relate to health and development is complex. We can't lump all screens together (watching a movie is different from building a world in an interactive game, which is different from blasting zombies with a console). What kids are watching, for how long, at what age, and in what context all matter.

We do have some information to help us make good choices, though. For example, we know that baby brains are programmed to learn from experimenting with the *physical world*. Infants learn physics from simple activities like rolling a ball and banging spoons; numbers and math concepts by putting blocks into a container or building a tower; and language from adults making eye contact, gesturing, and interacting as they talk. It's not just babies; little kids learn from the physical world too, and from having unstructured playtime in which they can create imaginary worlds, develop relationships, make plans, and follow through on ideas. Screen time is not necessarily bad, but for little kids, most other activities (even rolling around in the grass or snow) are better. The question of whether babies and little kids can learn from media and screens continues to be researched—it's likely that they can learn from quality educational media, especially when adults watch and interact along with them.

SCREENS AND BMI

Increased screen time is associated with higher body mass index and obesity rates. Again, it's hard to tease out which comes first, screens or sedentary tendencies. Screen time can also lead to mindless eating out of habit and consumption of higher-calorie snacks (which many of us adults can empathize with!).

In our experience, though, most parents don't use screens this way. They (understandably) turn on a screen while they take a break to do house chores, eat quickly, or take a shower. In that case, the latest recommendations from the American Academy of Pediatrics are to avoid the use of screen media, other than video chatting, for children younger than eighteen months; and for toddlers between eighteen and twenty-four months to choose high-quality programming and apps, and to interact with the child when using them. Between ages two and five years, the recommendation is to limit screen time to one hour per day of high-quality programming.

Primed for Meltdowns

Many of the video games on the market today are masterpieces of entertainment. They're immersive, they're exciting, they feel as though they should never end. When kids play, the world falls away and their minds are swept up. The nervous system goes on high alert—a dragon, a ninja, the next level, a pile of gold! Neurochemicals like dopamine are released, leading to a feel-good state and a desire to keep going. Many games even encourage frequent checking in and use so as not to miss out on extra points or benefits that arise randomly.

When it's over, other activities can seem less interesting and enjoyable. Stress hormones that raged during the epic dragon battle still course through the body. Sometimes video games can leave kids feeling mentally depleted and emotionally dysregulated. This can appear as a child being withdrawn, bored, or tantrum-prone. Parents tell us that their otherwise rational child is practically unrecognizable when it comes to screens. Other parents report what looks like a cycle of behavior problems and screen use: Kids who have trouble sitting still and regulating emotions are sometimes given screens to distract, soothe, and calm them down. In turn, when the screens go off, the problem has compounded.

This may sound like we're saying video games are bad, but the issue isn't one-dimensional. For example, research also shows that action video games can improve certain aspects of attention and multitasking ability. Precisely those powers that make video games so powerful can also be used for good. Video games are being developed to improve certain brain functions and elevate learning. There are many companies developing games that are constructive and teach skills. Not surprisingly, research shows that most parents of older children agree that technology positively supports their kids with schoolwork and education, and that technology helps them learn new skills and prepares them for future jobs.

So media and screens are powerful and multidimensional. It helps to be aware of how they affect your child's emotions and behaviors; to choose family screen practices that take good care of eating and sleep; and to protect time for unstructured play in the real world. Again, our focus in this chapter is to move beyond deeming screens as good or bad, and to help you think about their role in your family and their effect on your particular child. After you make decisions about family rules and habits around screens, we'll help you navigate common stuck moments and conversations about their use.

Attune

We all know screens can elicit big feelings for kids. Your baby might scream when you turn off her favorite television program, or your second-grader might sulk when you insist on the video game going off. No matter what the scenario, even if the emotions seem completely unreasonable (you *agreed* on only thirty more minutes!), it's important to attune to these feelings in the moment. When you attune, your little one feels understood. Even if she doesn't like the limit she will be more likely to listen to it when you listen to her too. See the scripts later in this chapter for examples.

ARE YOU THE ONE ON A DEVICE?

If you're the one looking at a screen and your child wants your attention, use your words and body language to show you're interested, even if you're busy. Touch your child's hand or head and say something like:

Ooh, wait, I really want to hear what you're saying, so let me finish this important message so I can really get this. I'm excited to hear it; give me two minutes.

Kids coming out of video game land may seem extra irrational and irritable. It's as if they're in withdrawal. This can be really hard for parents. If your child has been playing for two hours and you've given her five warnings, it's difficult to empathize with the sorrow and protest that can come when the game finally goes off. It may help to think about your child's brain and the previous description of how games can truly affect chemistry—your child's reactions are valid (it doesn't mean you should delay or go back on your limits).

An important way to attune around screens is to build a foundation that brings the family together, rather than pitting you against each other. This means attuning to your child's interests, thoughts, and feelings about her shows and games in regular moments—not just when they become a problem. This will set a better foundation of "we're on the same team" that will help you get through the moments of conflict that inevitably come up on the often contentious subject of screens. Here are ways to do this.

Ask, Watch, and Play

If you're worried about screen time, this may sound counterintuitive, but we want you to make friends with screens. The media content our kids watch is captivating to them, and it's running around their minds long after the screens go off. You have a chance to engage and help them make sense of it. If you simply endure a certain amount, demand the TV or games go off, and never speak about it, you're missing an opportunity.

Align with your child and try to understand what he likes about what he's watching or playing. If you talk about media as the bad guy, you'll be an outsider because you "don't get it."

- Ask questions about what your child is playing. How does the game work? How do you get to the next level?

- Ask what he thinks is fun about it. Don't be afraid to talk about how cool a certain show is—you want your child to feel like you respect his passion.
- Talk about how he feels when he plays.
- Try to understand the game and play it yourself. Get a second game console and play with your child. This will surely help you empathize with him about what makes them so great.

Limit Set

Limits for Kids

Don't Be Afraid to Censor Content

It's helpful to use tools like Common Sense Media to see what's appropriate for certain age groups, but make choices just for your family. That might mean you're okay with certain things, like explicit lyrics in a song, that other families may not allow, but that you are not okay with violent shows. Or you might know that your children aren't fazed by cartoon aggression, but that they are sensitive to heartbreak and emotionally heavy story lines in a movie. Maybe the characters of a given show call each other names or the values of the show don't align with your own. Kids learn from what they watch, and that includes the vocabulary, tone, and mannerisms of the characters. Most adults can still remember certain images or stories that upset them or were too intense for them as children. There's no value in exposing kids to media content that upsets or frightens them, with the idea that it will "toughen them up." One of the best ways to know the content of the show is to watch together.

GOOD TO STEER CLEAR OF . . .

Fast-paced programs and apps with distracting or busy sensory content are too much for little kids. Research suggests that quick edits and disconnected or fast story lines can overload the brain's executive function and make it harder for kids to focus and self-regulate. If you find a certain program or app loud, annoying, or busy, it's probably not good for little minds.

Avoid Using Devices to Distract and Soothe

It's tempting to use screens as a distraction if your toddler is getting frustrated or crying and complaining, but this is a slippery slope. Babies and little kids need connection, eye contact, and physical touch—this is how they develop self-regulation and a secure attachment. This doesn't mean you can never have a "911" moment when a screen saves you, but using screens quickly becomes a habit and little ones come to expect it. We really want our babies and kids to get the message that their "negative" feelings are fine with us and that we're not trying to immediately make them go away. Using screens to soothe little ones can quickly become a cycle, because the more screens are used to distract them, the less practice they get self-regulating and the more acting out and other difficult moments will happen.

Set Child Screen Limits at Family Meetings, and Hold Them

It's much easier on children if we set up screen limits and rules at a family meeting, rather than making up rules on the fly. This makes your children part of the process, allowing them to brainstorm and give their input too (a three-year-old should be involved in family meetings, even if her contribution is to talk about the princess kite that got caught in a tree one time). When you decide on your family agreements around screens, stick to them. This will make it easier for you to hold limits and it will make the limits clear and trustworthy to your children. If the family agreement is one hour of screen time per day, try as much as you can not to bend or change this rule. If you consistently hold to it, your children will trust the limit (even if they don't like it).

Limits for the Family

Phones and Devices off When You Eat

Turning off and putting away electronics and media before you eat supports mindful eating and allows the family to talk and connect. This applies to restaurants too. It's easy to hand a toddler a device at the dinner table to occupy her. Will giving a screen to a toddler in a restaurant to occupy her be harmful to her? No. Will she expect to watch a screen the next time you're at dinner? Very likely. If you can hold good, reasonable restaurant expectations and stay clear about electronics and eating, you'll set a precedent that your kids will always trust. Remember, you have to adhere to the agreement too!

Limit Background Television

Research suggests that background television interferes with family interactions: babies and toddlers interact less with their parents and have a lower quality of interaction when the TV is on. It also suggests that kids have a hard time focusing and playing well when television is on (even if they're not watching the television). No one wants to miss their favorite team's game, but it's important to be choosy about when the TV is on.

Put Away Devices with Purpose

Rather than having multiple devices out, in eyesight, all over the house, have kids and parents put them in a particular place when they're done. Devices might live on a bookshelf, in a drawer, or on an office desk—not on the coffee table or dinner table, and especially not in bedrooms. Having a space to park devices out of direct eyesight helps symbolically turn them off and shift attention to other activities. It makes the boundary between screen time and not-screen-time clearer.

Limits for You

Imagine you're playing with your baby on the floor, swinging her on the swings, or changing her diaper when your phone pings. You turn your head and reach for your device, maybe even for a thirty-second update. This happens dozens or even hundreds of times every day. Babies and little kids grow up with us dividing our attention constantly. Try not to think of this as a black-and-white, good–bad issue—electronic devices allow us to research, learn, and work with mobility, and allow our kids to have advantages like video chatting with a parent or grandparent who's not there.

You have the opportunity to model and teach a healthy relationship with devices. This is a relationship that will be passed to your child through modeling, just as with other healthy habits like those around eating and sleeping. Practice limit setting with yourself. Rather than feeling guilty about devices, you can be mindful of your behaviors and consciously choose how you relate to them, rather than letting them control you.

NARRATE WHAT YOU'RE DOING ON YOUR DEVICE

Most of the time kids don't know what we're doing when we look at devices. It's not the newspaper, it's not the telephone—it doesn't have a clear purpose from the outside. It's an undefined place where our attention is continually drawn. We can help our kids not feel quite so on the outside by defining what we're doing. Say,

I'm arranging the carpool for tomorrow.

I'm checking the game schedule.

I'm going to look up the answer to that question here.

Out of Sight, Out of Mind

Choose times when you put your phone completely away, out of sight, so you're less likely to think about it (the ringer could be on so you still get phone calls). If you walk your child to school in the morning, can you make it a device-free daily walk? Make mealtimes device free—parking phones and turning off electronics before coming to the table.

If you're working from home or waiting for an important phone call, then you may need your phone next to you, but if not, can you put it up on a bookshelf until you need it? Turn your alerts down or off. Save personalized rings and tones that allow you to screen what you want to answer.

Here is a sample of family screen rules. Look at chapter 2 on running a family meeting, and make these your own!

OUR FAMILY SCREEN AGREEMENTS

For the kids, the weekdays are screen free. Exceptions include computers needed for homework and special events like sports finals.

Eating is special family time. At the table, we eat, talk, and laugh. Kids and grown-ups do not have screens or phones during mealtime (at home or in restaurants).

Screens go to bed before we do. No phones or computers in the bedroom. We turn off all screens (that's parents too!) one hour before we climb into bed.

We have a list of shows and video games that are okay to watch and play. If we want to add something to the list, Mom or Dad has to watch it and see if it's okay to add.

Problem Solve

Turning off screens is a transition, and transitions can be hard for everybody—big and small. Some kids react extra strongly to having screens taken away, because their brains are wildly absorbed in what they're doing. You probably know how this goes, as if there's nothing more important and desired in the whole world. Turning off screens is a massive injustice!

You'll see examples in the upcoming scripts section for problem solving with screens. If your child is too upset about turning off a screen or adhering to a family rule about screens (like not having them at the table), you may have to simply hold the limit and wait until he's receptive enough to think creatively or to be more flexible.

For now, you are the one setting screen rules and limits, but you won't always be looking over his shoulder to see what he's watching and make him turn screens off. Our ultimate goal is to help our kids become critical thinkers and smart media consumers. This takes many forms; for example:

Rather than just tell your preschooler she can't watch a certain show, explain your thinking behind it.

> *This isn't a show we watch, because it doesn't have any information in it.*

> *This isn't a show we watch, because it's too fast and overwhelming to our minds.*

> *This isn't a show we watch, because the characters call each other names.*

We only watch one hour of TV each day so we can leave room in the day and in our minds for everything else: running, building, talking, playing—we have to keep space for those things.

If you are watching a show or playing a game, encourage critical thinking. Help your child see how games work and why they're so tempting and engaging.

Whoa, I wonder how that character felt when she said that. What do you think?

Is this show too intense? It's feeling really intense to me!

How did you feel when you got to that level? How did you feel when you didn't make the next level?

Can you see how that game is tricking your mind to think you have to keep playing? Games are very good at keeping us playing!

If you feel as though your family rules around screens are not working, bring this up at a family meeting, to brainstorm and problem solve together. Be sure to listen and consider what your kids are telling you, while also holding on to all the knowledge and wisdom you have about what is best for their growing minds.

Scripts and Conversations

Scripts

Baby

SCENARIO: *You turn off your baby's favorite show.*

PREPARATION	ATTUNE	LIMIT SET	PROBLEM SOLVE
The show is almost over. *(The show ends.)* We're turning off the show. Bye-bye, Thomas!	You're sad the show is over. I see you're crying, sweetie.	The show is over now so we turned it off.	I'm turning on some fun music. *(Or)* Let's have a sip of water and a snack.

Toddler/Preschooler

SCENARIO: *You're at a restaurant and your child sees another child watching something on her parent's phone.*

PREPARATION	ATTUNE	LIMIT SET	PROBLEM SOLVE
We're heading to a restaurant, so hey, can anyone tell me what our restaurant rules are? Yes! Who's got another one?	I know, you see a friend watching a movie at the table. You feel like that looks fun.	In our family we don't watch screens at the table. That gives us the chance to focus on eating, talking, and being together.	I have that pack of markers and I actually got a new coloring book this week. Let's use them until the food comes out.

Conversations

Changing a Screen Rule

Mommy and I realized that watching screens in the morning is not working well for the family. We think it might be waking your brain up too early in the morning, and also we want to protect morning time for other things. That means we'll do our usual morning steps—eating breakfast, talking, playing, getting dressed. In the afternoon we'll make time for screens.

What? Noooooo! I want to play. Just ten minutes? Five minutes?

I know, it's fun and you were expecting to watch. This is our new screen setup, though. We know it's the best way for everyone, even though it doesn't feel like it right in this moment.

It's not good for me! That's not fair. Please? I just have to check my game. Just check. Two minutes.

It sounds like a short amount of time, but it's not about how long you're on the game. We aren't playing games in the morning. You can put the screen back on the shelf, or I can do it for you. I promise it'll be there and ready for you later.

(Child starts to sulk.) *This sucks.*

I hear ya. Can you remember to bring it up at our family meeting and share any ideas you have?

CHAPTER EIGHT

Bedtime and Sleep

Sleep is an essential part of life—but more important, sleep is a gift.

—**William C. Dement, MD**

It's the end of the day and your toddler is running naked laps around the house. Your older child refuses to get out of the bath. You chase the little one down and wrestle him into pajamas, while the older one finally stands dripping on the carpet, waiting to be dried. They act like you're suggesting torture when you say it's time to brush teeth. As soon as teeth are brushed, one remembers a piece of homework that is *very important* to do for tomorrow and wanders off to spill out the contents of his backpack again. The little one starts crying that he's suddenly, and desperately, hungry and needs a snack.

Many moms and dads dread this time of the day. Parents tell us all the time how frustrated they feel as the evening rolls in and their kids wind up. There are ten steps to do before bed, no one listens, and they basically can't wait for the whole thing to be over. We've worked with thousands of families on sleep issues, and almost all of them stem, in some way or another, from what happens in the steps leading up to sleep.

Often parents' frustration, very understandably, comes out in the words they say and the tone they use about sleep. Here are examples of common phrases we hear before bed:

Bed, now!

You have to go to bed!

Get in bed, right now.

If you don't get your pajamas on, you're going straight to bed with no dessert.

Forget it, no stories tonight. Go straight to bed!

You're cranky. Do you need to go night-night?

These words may sound mild, but they contain some pretty negative messages about sleep. With this language, sleep is a consequence or a dreaded end. It's not a great place to go, or a time to look forward to. Some parents might even send their child to his bed or crib for a time-out if he's broken a rule.

We know *you* don't think of sleep as negative (or, if you do, it's time to examine your own ideas about sleep!). Most likely, you feel like sleep is a welcome place to go and you probably look forward to it yourself. Sleep is lovely. Sleep is a luxury.

We wrote an entire book full of strategies to help children (newborn through school age) establish healthy sleep habits, sleep through the night, take good naps, and more. If you want help with these topics and specific guidance please read our book *The Happy Sleeper*. We can't solve specific sleep problems in this chapter, but if you're like the families we hear from every day, our sleep book will do the trick.

In this chapter, we're going to help you reposition sleep in your house, using language and tone. Sleep should be a priority—it's essential for your child's health and happiness, and yours too—and it can be a time that everyone looks forward to and has positive feelings about. A family that sleeps well has more energy for each other during the day, when life's challenges will always arise. It's almost impossible to communicate well when you or your child is sleep deprived. With sleep on your side, everyone is more creative and patient.

How Much Sleep Do You Really Need?

Age	Sleep Needs
Newborns (0-2 months)	12-18 hours
Infants (3-11 months)	14 to 15 hours
Toddlers (1-3 years)	12 to 14 hours
Preschoolers (3-5 years)	11 to 13 hours
School-age children (5-10 years)	10 to 11 hours
Teens (10-17 years)	8.5 - 9.25 hours
Adults	7-9 hours

Connected, Capable, and Cozy

When it comes to sleep, babies and children need to feel what we call the three Cs: connected, capable, and cozy. They need to feel *connected*, which means we acknowledge their needs and they can say good night knowing we're nearby. They need us to believe they are *capable*, which means we keep clear expectations and family practices around sleep. Finally, they need a *cozy*, optimal sleeping environment.

This chapter is structured slightly differently from the others (although it too has scripts and conversations using ALP at the end). We will address certain aspects of the three Cs, like creating a positive atmosphere around sleep, establishing wind-down and bedtime routines, and important elements of the bedroom environment that promote healthy sleep. We'll give you examples of language and conversations and share ways to promote a warm, positive climate around bedtime. If you need specific help with sleep issues (for example, a child waking in the night, having trouble with naps, not falling asleep independently, and more), please refer to *The Happy Sleeper*. Methods from that book are incredibly successful for babies, toddlers and school-age kids.

Balanced Days Lead to Better Sleep

Stressful days can lead to fitful nights. Lots of parents and kids are overscheduled and frantic with activities and responsibilities. There's no simple trick for solving this dilemma—and as busy, ambitious people ourselves, we wouldn't even say that being very active and involved is a bad thing. Both of us are working parents, and our kids work hard, get involved in clubs, and are dedicated to sports. Our homes are busy too!

At the same time, when life feels out of balance, it's harder for kids to relax and for their biology to support a long night of good-quality sleep. Saying good night also requires confidence and peace of mind, which is created through connection during the day. Rest assured, this is more about quality than quantity. Even busy working parents who don't have much time to spend with their kids each day can give their kids a sense of connection. Get down on eye level to say good-bye, give a hug, and tell your child to keep that hug "in your pocket" for during the day when you're thinking of each other.

Snuggle on the couch together, even for ten minutes before bed, and share your highs and lows of the day. Video chat with the parent who isn't there for bedtime. Leave a note in your child's lunch box. It's the quality that our kids feel—this is part of what creates a secure attachment and a sense that they can go out into the world (and also disconnect at night) with confidence.

There are a lot of ways to create a less stressful day; for example:

- Limit playdates after school to once or twice a week. That is, unless playdates create *less* stress for you, and your children are still able to be home early enough to eat and have wind-down time (see page 304).
- Have kids choose one sport or activity at a time.
- Arrange carpools.
- Grocery shop with meals planned for at least a few nights.
- Have groceries delivered.
- Ask grandparents, friends, and neighbors for help. Most people understand and you will have a chance to help them or someone else in return down the road.
- Limit weekday screen time. This sounds counterintuitive, because many parents use screen time as a reward or a chance to get chores done. If weekday screen time makes life easier, that's fine, but really consider it: Do screens create power struggles and meltdowns? Are your kids focused on screens and unable to find enjoyment in building, running, and creating games of their own? Kids need unstructured time playing in the physical world. When they don't have it, they feel less regulated and peaceful.
- Embrace boredom. Help your kids enjoy doing nothing,

daydreaming, lying in the grass, or whatever comes up when there isn't a structured activity.

- Look at page 204 for suggestions on structuring chores and to-do lists.
- Practice the mindfulness exercises in chapter 2.

Wind-Down Time Shifts the Brain into Sleep-Ready Mode

The hour leading up to bedtime is when your child's mind and body should be shifting. You don't see it happening, but under the surface, the body is preparing for sleep. Lots of parents we work with expect their kids to go from playdates, screens, homework, and more and move straight into their bedtime routines. This often doesn't work, and kids have a hard time clicking over immediately into teeth, books, and popping into bed (unless they're exhausted, which we don't want). It can also cause them to have disrupted sleep or wake up too early in the morning.

This is why we implement "wind-down time" for our families. Wind-down time is different from the bedtime routine. It simply means parents are helping their kids' minds and bodies shift gears. Wind-down time is a *feeling*, not a particular activity—you can create your own and it might change night to night (whereas bedtime routines should stay the same).

1. **Try to be home for an hour before bed.** Coming in the door and immediately getting into pajamas might be fine on the occasional Saturday night after an evening with friends. Most nights, though, it helps for kids to be home for wind-down time.

2. **Turn down the lights, draw the curtains.** Light, especially sunlight, bright white light, and blue light, suppresses the release of mel-

atonin, which your child needs to become drowsy and fall asleep. For at least one hour before bedtime, turn off bright overhead lights and close curtains in the summer.

3. **No screens.** On page 283 you'll find an explanation of why screens interfere with sleep. At least one hour before bed (we prefer it to be at least two hours) should be screen free.

4. **Lower your voice, avoid stressful talks, put your own devices away.** Whoever is home with the kids during wind-down time could be doing anything—prepping lunches for the next day, folding laundry, listening to music, drawing with the kids—but it should be relatively relaxing. This relaxation is absorbed by your kids. Put away your phone and computer if you can. This allows you to connect with your kids, which in turn makes them more open to moving through the steps of the routine. They've filled up on you, so they can now disconnect and fall asleep. Enjoying each other before bed makes saying good night feel good. This can take a deep well of patience and some advanced planning on your part. Read page 81 if you find yourself getting very stressed or reacting with anger before bed.

The Bedtime Routine Cues the Brain for Sleep

The steps leading up to your baby's or child's bedtime, whether they take just fifteen minutes or forty-five, should stay consistent night to night. If you have the exact same bedtime routine, after a few nights it makes it easier for your child to fall asleep (this goes for you too—parents also need small bedtime routines). Bedtime routines can be anything calming. They should include tending to physical needs, like taking a bath and brushing teeth, and also activities that your child enjoys, or you enjoy together, like reading books, singing songs, and child-led play. Even babies need social activities in their bedtime routines, and many times when we do sleep consultations with parents of babies we see these social elements missing.

WHAT'S THE BEST SLEEP SCHEDULE FOR MY CHILD?

The best sleep schedules for little kids are early and regular. As parents of babies and little kids know, most children are early risers. They can be ready to start the day at 6:00 a.m. In our online sleep classes, we put it this way: Let's say you put a child to bed at 7:00 p.m. and she wakes up at 6:00 a.m. If you put the same child to bed at 9:00 p.m., what time will she wake? Most parents answer 6:00 a.m.! This is usually true. Babies and small kids are programmed to wake up early and have strong internal alarms. They have the best chance of getting a full night's sleep if they have an early bedtime. Babies and little kids need eleven to twelve hours of nighttime sleep, and school-age children need ten to eleven hours of nighttime sleep.

Kids also thrive on regularity. This is a fact about how the human body works. The internal clock helps us anticipate and regulate many of our behaviors and states, like eating and sleep. When kids (and grown-ups too) go to bed and wake up at the same time each day, they're working with the body's natural inclination for schedule. We fall asleep more easily, feel better, think and learn better, and have more patience and greater powers of emotional regulation.

Establish an early bedtime and keep it the same every night of the week (rather than staying up late on the weekends). Of course there will always be exceptions to the rule, but try to make early bedtimes the norm.

The Right Words Engage Cooperation in the Bedtime Routine

If your kids are not getting ready for bed, try not to criticize, threaten, or yell.

Instead of:

Why are you not listening to me?

You're so slow!

Get your pajamas on, now!

If you don't put your pj's on you're not going to the birthday party this weekend. Is that what you want?

Go brush your teeth or you're going to time-out!

You can state realities in a matter-of-fact way:

Anyone know what our next step is here? Where's the list of bedtime steps?

Let's get our steps done so we can climb in bed and read.

The clock is telling us it's time for a bath.

Use natural enticements:

Let's do our teeth so we can have lots of time for reading. I'm excited to hear what happens next.

When your teeth are brushed and jammies are on, we'll climb into bed and do our highs and lows of the day.

Position sleep as a welcome treat:

Come on, let's get cozy!

After you guys climb into bed, I can't wait to snuggle up with my book.

Let's all go to bed a little early tonight and fill up on sleep.

Is your pillow cozy? Lemme climb in and lay my head on it to check. Oh, that's nice.

The bedtime routine goes more smoothly if there's something kids look forward to at the end. That could be as simple as the next chapter of a book, a shadow puppet show with a flashlight when they climb into bed, or anything else that motivates.

FROM HEATHER: THE BACKRUB CHAIN

My kids have had different bedtime routines as they've grown, and often it's the next chapter of a book they're interested in reading (and me too—we choose books we're all excited to read), but recently I taught them how to do a backrub chain. We sit one in front of the other and the person rubbing someone's back asks, Would they like tickles, massage, or what? After a minute, the front person moves to the back. It's really sweet. They think it's fun (but it's relaxing too), and it's definitely a way for us to all connect before bedtime.

The Pitfalls of the Sticker Chart

After a preschool sleep class one evening, a sweet dad approached us and said, "This thing about language makes so much sense! I get it. Tonight I'm going to start talking differently about sleep." This all sounded great, except that he followed up with, "So should I put up a reward chart? Every time she stays in bed, she gets a star, and she gets a prize at the end of the week?" Woops. We realized that "positive" messaging can be misinterpreted. As with other realms of life, heavily praising can backfire. If you lay on the rewards and praise over sleep, it could get you through a stuck moment, but in the long run, this doesn't contribute to a healthy relationship to sleep.

How praise can backfire, and what to say instead.

The Sleeping Environment Promotes Quality Sleep

We could write a whole chapter on the sleeping environment (ask the parents in our classes and consultations—we love to talk about it!), because it's such a powerful force. A smart, thoughtful bedroom makes all the difference.

1. **Dark.** Harness the power of light and dark to promote sleep. The bedroom should be completely dark from the last step of the bedtime routine (also for naps) until your child's optimal wake-up time and. Use darkening shades and blackout curtains. Do not have electronics with lights in the bedroom at night. Light is activating to the brain and sends wake-up signals.

2. **Cool.** The optimal sleeping temperature is sixty-five to sixty-eight degrees. That's cooler than most parents keep their baby's or child's bedroom. It doesn't mean you need to crank up the air conditioner in the summer, but it does mean you should set a lower temperature for heat in the winter. You can also use a fan to create moving air in the bedroom.

3. **Quiet.** Use white noise on a low volume. We like slightly variable noises like rain or waves, but any sound that is constant and low during the night (such as a low fan or air purifier) will help muffle noises from inside and outside the house and protect sleep.

4. **Peaceful.** Kids' rooms are often also playrooms, so it's hard to keep them uncluttered, but if you can—if toys are minimal, and put away and stored for sleep—it helps kids feel relaxed and associate the room with sleeping.

Bedtime Routine Chart

Bath								
Brush teeth								
Pajamas								
Storytime								
Potty								
Lights out								
Songs								
Hugs + Kisses								

"Collecting Frogs"

Heather's friend called her one morning to vent about her kids' bed-time routine. "They don't listen to me and I end up so frustrated every night. I get one of the three of them close to bed, then turn around and the other two have gotten out of the bedroom. I get them back and then the other one won't brush his teeth. I'm standing there after saying six times to my son to put his pajamas on, and he's star-ing at me lazily without doing it. It drives me crazy! It's like I'm try-ing to collect frogs in a corner: I get one there and then one hops out." As her friend talked, she realized how tense she was, and that it was making bedtime unpleasant. Her son, the middle child, who used to always ask her to cuddle before bed, no longer did. "He knows I'm so frustrated, he doesn't ask me to snuggle anymore. I feel like I'm losing my kid," she worried. She felt like it was her job to change the tone around bedtime. One day, when everyone was calm during the day, she met with her husband and the son who had the most trouble get-ting ready before bed. "Something's not working before bed, can you guys tell?" She asked for ideas. Her son said he wanted to be in charge and didn't want anyone telling him what to do. His mom and dad said that was okay, as long as he took responsibility for keeping track of his pre-bed steps. They printed a list of things that needed to happen before tucking into bed. They decided the parents would only give reminders about the time, like "Check your list," or "Hey, I just no-ticed it's almost eight o'clock. Just checking—I know you like to have your backpack packed up before bed." When the son was in bed, they had cuddle time and would talk about their highs and lows of the day. It became like a game to get into bed by 8:15. That natural re-ward, along with the feeling of responsibility and team cooperation, was enough to motivate the son to move along in his steps. The par-ents stopped yelling and the enjoyment of nighttime went back up.

Scripts and Conversations

Scripts

SCENARIO: *The kids are running around and not moving into their bedtime routine.*

PREPARE	ATTUNE	LIMIT SET	PROBLEM SOLVE
In five minutes, we'll get into pj's. Everyone do your last thing.	Oh, man, we're all super energetic right now! I'm putting on some wind-down music.	It's time for pj's.	Anyone need help with theirs, or you got it? *(Or)* Anyone need an airplane lift to the bedroom?

Conversations

Your Child Gets Stuck
During the Bedtime Routine.

Time for pajamas.

I can't get into pajamas. I'm working on this drawing! (Sitting in a chair, starts to cry.)

Oh, I see. (Dad comes over and gets down under child's eye level.) *Yes, I can see what you're working on. It's an intricate drawing. It's not finished yet, huh?*

No, and if I don't finish it, I'll forget and I'll never finish it!

You worry if you don't finish it now, you'll never finish it.

Yesssssss!

Hmm, well, let's see. (**Pause.**) *It's time for bed, so what could we do?*

Keep drawing till I finish!

Only that's not going to work since it's almost time for stories and bed. Hmm.

Draw for one more minute.

That sounds like it would work. Should I tell you when a minute is up?

Yes.

This conversation has two endings. In the first, when the dad gives her the "one minute's up," the little one puts away her drawing and brushes her teeth. In the alternate ending, it doesn't go so smoothly:

Okay, one minute is up. Meet you in the bathroom for teeth!

No! One more minute! I have to finish.

It's hard to put it down.

Yes, I can not. (Starts to cry again.)

It looks like it's really hard to stop. I'm going to help you, okay? Do you want to put the drawing down on the bookshelf so you can finish it tomorrow, or should I do it? (The dad is not using a scolding or threatening voice, just a matter-of-fact "I'm going to help you" voice. He has to take a deep breath to do this!)

Okay, I'm helping. Here, I'm taking the drawing so you can go to your next step. (This is a follow-through step.)

Saying Good Night With Confidence.

In this conversation the mom has made a new, very clear sleep plan (from *The Happy Sleeper*), she's shared the plan with her daughter, and then she checks in about how the first night went.

You like your zoo ones, huh? They're in the laundry, so we're wearing the train pj's. Okay, so we're tucked in here. Remember, when the lights go out and I say good night, you're in charge of your own body and your own stuff.

I have my sippy cup of water on my table.

Yup, and you have your favorite stuffed animal. What would you do if your blanket fell off in the night? Let's practice pulling it up.

I'd pull it at the top and put it back under my chin. And grab Doggie.

Wow, you really know what to do.

Instead Of "Good Job" Or "Bad Job."

I noticed it was hard to stay in your bed last night. You were really upset. I checked on you, but kept taking you back to your own bed, just like we planned.

I want to sleep with you!

I hear you. It seems nice to sleep with me, and we used to do that. This feels different. But it's my job to help you sleep, and now we have a new plan. Let's remember it together. When the sun goes down and the moon comes out, we all go to sleep in our own beds. When the sun comes up in the morning, we see each other and play.

Acknowledgments

Thank you to our editor, Sara Carder, for believing in us; to Heather Brennan for shepherding us through this process; and to our agent, Michelle Tessler, for her advice and insight.

Thank you to friends, family, and colleagues who read and gave us feedback on this book: Amy Dickens, Laurel Garber, Ben Hansford, KimLan Kala, Brynn Karwas, Jennifer McNamara, Mary Posatko, Christine Richard, Jane Rosen, Rana Shanawani, Gillian Turgeon, Robert Turgeon, Michelle Villemaire, and Rosie Willis.

We have learned so much from researchers and clinicians such as Stanley Greenspan, Alfie Kohn, Dan Siegel, Tina Bryson, John Bowlby, Lise Eliot, Cindy Hazan, Jon Kabat-Zinn, Adele Faber, and Elaine Mazlish.

From Heather:

Thank you to my husband for being our number one book champion, for capturing the essence of our ideas so beautifully in drawings (I knew you would). Most of all, thank you for nodding and saying, "I get it. Tell me more . . ."

I couldn't write about this way of raising kids without feeling it in my heart, where I have my own parents' unconditional love. Thank you for always listening and having open arms. And to my amazing little sister, whose relationship with my kids brings us all endless joy.

Thank you to my kids for brainstorming ideas, techniques, and titles with me. You gave this book its character. Thank you both for your empathic way and for articulating your feelings. I'm the luckiest person in the world that I get to hug and talk to you both every day.

From Julie:

I have long been fascinated by how leading with empathy can turn a difficult, distressing moment into one of deeper understanding and connection. I have many to thank.

My professors at Antioch University and my supervisors at my internships at Cedars-Sinai Early Childhood and LA Child Guidance Clinic supported and expanded my understanding immeasurably.

All of the parents, babies and class leaders in my mommy and me program were instrumental as I sought to simplify the inspiring field of mindful parenting into a simple and user-friendly approach. ALP was the end result, and I couldn't have done it without all of you.

I observe and listen to people constantly (kindness is everywhere if you look for it) and try out ALP whenever I can. Thank you to all the strangers out there who have demonstrated empathy and responded positively to a kind, understanding word from me.

It all started with my precious family. My mom, whose love is unconditional, taught us early on that there was no dilemma we couldn't talk through and to never go to bed angry. My dad, who died fourteen years ago, was a thoughtful, kind, and gentle soul. He had the patience of a saint and was also a natural teacher. My sister and two brothers (Susan, David, and Stephen) along with our extended family, have always been there to listen, love, and support me. My number one teacher has been my son Jack, who always beamed when I was empathic and let me know when I was not. He allowed me to circle back and repair over and over. He is one of the kindest people I'm proud to know.

Notes

Chapter 1

Babies' moral sense

Hamlin, J. K., Wynn, K., & Bloom, P. (2010). "Three-month-olds show a negativity bias in their social evaluations." *Developmental Science* 13(6), 1–7.

Parenting styles

Chang, L., Schwartz, D., Dodge, K. A., McBride-Chang, C. (2003). "Harsh parenting in relation to child emotion regulation and aggression." *Journal of Family Psychology* 17(4), 598–606.

Wang, M. T., & Kenny, S. (2014). "Longitudinal links between fathers' and mothers' harsh verbal discipline and adolescents' conduct problems and depressive symptoms." *Child Development* 85(3), 908–23.

Gershoff, E. T., et al. (2010). "Parent discipline practices in an international sample: associations with child behaviors and moderation by perceived normativeness." *Child Development* 81(2), 487–502.

Spera, C. (2005). "A review of the relationship among parenting practices, parenting styles, and adolescent school achievement." *Educational Psychology Review* 17(2), 125–46.

Denham, S. A. (2000). "Prediction of externalizing behavior problems from early to middle childhood: the role of parental socialization and emotion expression." *Developmental Psychopathology* 12(1), 23–45.

Gottman, J. M., Fainsilber Katz, L., Hooven, C. (1996). "Parental meta-emotion philosophy and the emotional life of families: theoretical models and preliminary data." *Journal of Family Psychology* 10(3), 243–68.

Rewards lower intrinsic motivation

Deci, E. L., Koestner, R., Ryan, R. M. (1999). "A meta-analytic review of experiments examining the effects of extrinsic rewards on intrinsic motivation." *Psychological Bulletin* 125(6), 627–68.

Rowe, M. B. (1974). "Relation of wait time and rewards to the development of language, logic, and fate control: Part II—rewards." *Journal of Research in Science Teaching* 11(4), 291–308.

Chapter 2

Effects of exercise on the brain

Best, J. R. (2010). "Effects of physical activity on children's executive function: contributions of experimental research on aerobic exercise." *Developmental Review* 30(4), 331–51.

Shevtsova, O., Tan, Y., Merkley, C. M., Winocur, G., Wojtowicz, J. M. (2017). "Early-age running enhances activity of adult-born dentate granule neurons following learning in rats." eNeuro.

Oppezzo, M., Schwartz, D. L. (2014). "Give your ideas some legs: the positive effect of walking on creative thinking." *Journal of Experimental Psychology: Learning, Memory, and Cognition* 40(4), 1142–52.

Nature and the brain

Van Den Berg, A. E., Custers, M. H. (2011). "Gardening promotes neuroendocrine and affective restoration from stress." *Journal of Health Psychology* 16(1), 3–11.

Chapter 4

Sadeh, A., Gruber, R., Raviv, A. (2003). "The effects of sleep restriction and extension on school-age children: what a difference an hour makes." *Child Development* 74(2), 444–55.

Palmer, C.A., Alfano, C.A. (2017). "Sleep and emotion regulation: An organizing, integrative review." *Sleep Medicine Reviews* 31, 6–16.

Chapter 7

Parents' technology distraction and its effects on kids

McDaniel, B. T., Radesky, J. S. (2018). "Technoference: parent distraction with technology and associations with child behavior problems." *Child Development* 89(1), 100–9.

Radesky, et al. (2014). "Maternal mobile device use during a structured parent-child interaction task." *Academic Pediatrics* 15(2), 238–44.

Video game effects

Bavelier, D., Green, C. S. (July 2016). "The brain-boosting power of video games." *Scientific American*, 28–31.

AAP Policy Statement on Screen Time: Media and Young Minds, October 2016.

Schmidt, M. E., Pempek, T. A., Kirkorian, H. L., Lund, A. F., Anderson, D. R. (2008). "The effects of background television on the toy-play behavior of very young children." *Child Development* 79(4), 1137–51.

Kirkorian, H. L., Pempek, T. A., Murphy, L. A., Schmidt, M. E., Anderson, D. R (2009). "The impact of background television on parent-child interaction." *Child Development* 80(5), 1350–9.

Falbe, et al. (2015). "Sleep duration, restfulness, and screens in the sleep environment." *Pediatrics* 135(2).

Garrison, M. M., Liekweg, K., Christakis, D. A. (2011). "Media use and child sleep: the impact of content, timing, and environment." *Pediatrics* 128(1), 29–35.

Foley, et al. (2013). "Presleep activities and time of sleep onset in children." Pediatrics 131(2), 276–82.

Common Sense Research: commonsensemedia.org/research.

Index

Note: Page numbers in *italics* refer to illustrations.